MAR 1 2

The Comeback

The Comeback

Seven Stories of Women Who Went from Career to Family and Back Again

Emma Gilbey Keller

BLOOMSBURY

Published by Bloomsbury USA, New York

All papers used by Bloomsbury USA are natural, recyclable products made from
wood grown in well-managed forests. The manufacturing processes conform to the
environmental regulations of the country of origin.

LIBRARY OF CONGRESS CATALOGING-IN-PUBLICATION DATA

Keller, Emma Gilbey
The comeback : seven stories of women who went from career to family
and back again / Emma Gilbey Keller.—1st U.S. ed.
p.   cm.
ISBN-13: 978-1-59691-223-6
ISBN-10: 1-59691-223-5
1. Women—Employment re-entry—United States—Case studies. 2. Women
in the professions—United States—Case studies. 3. Stay-at-home
mothers—United States—Case studies. 4. Work and family—United
States. I. Title.
HD6054. 2. U6K45 2008
331.4'4092273—dc22
2008004821

First U.S. Edition 2008

1   3   5   7   9   10   8   6   4   2

Typeset by Westchester Book Group
Printed in the United States of America by Quebecor World Fairfield

For Molly and Alice—the next generation

Contents

Introduction

You can have it all, but not all at once.

Arlene Cardozo

I WAS THIRTY-TWO when my first book was published in 1993. This is my second book. I haven't been working on it for fifteen years, but it does contain much of my experience from that time. To put it another way, if it weren't for those fifteen years, this book wouldn't exist.

My first book—a biography of Winnie Mandela—took me three years to write. During that time I did nothing but work on the book. No vacations, no romances, not much social life. My work was my world, and when it was published I felt a sense of loss as well as achievement. I used to tell people that handing in a book was my version of having a baby. I now had something concrete to show for all that gestation, but I was suffering from a little postpartum depression. I forced the metaphor still further by describing my book party as the equivalent of a wedding celebration. I remember getting dressed for it in a little black dress, black tights, and black heels and joking that it was cool to wear black instead of white. Instead of being married with children, I was celebrating being a successful single career woman. And that was fine. When you're thirty-two years old, that is absolutely fine.

I had always taken my work seriously, but until the book I had managed to have a vigorous social life as well. My first job in journalism was in the eighties at *Roll Call* newspaper in Washington, D.C., staffed mainly by twenty-somethings who didn't take themselves very seriously. The mandate of our weekly paper was to cover the Congress for the Congress. The mandate of our newsroom was to joke about the Congress for our own pleasure. My beat was to cover women members and wives of members. It was my idea. I wanted to explore the role of the wife in the changing world of late-twentieth-century Washington.

That same idea lay behind the appeal of covering Winnie Mandela's trial in South Africa in 1990. I had long left *Roll Call*, first to a brief stint in the press office of Al Gore's 1988 presidential campaign and then to ABC News's Washington bureau. By the time I got to South Africa at the end of 1989, I had decided to become a freelance journalist. I only wanted to write about what I was interested in. And Winnie Mandela's life incorporated everything I liked to cover— women, politics, and crime. Writing a book about her at the end of her trial was a logical next step.

When your work is your world and you fall in love, things have to change a little, sometimes a lot. When I fell in love with Bill Keller, who at the time was the foreign news editor of the *New York Times*, I had to learn how to make room. By then the book had been published and I was in demand as a feature writer. I lived alone in a small, very pretty, cottage in Sag Harbor, New York. I had an enormous view of the Long Island Sound from most windows, a fireplace, a cat, and a television. I still didn't have much of a social life. My assignments took me around the United States doing magazine pieces and stories for the *Sunday Times* of London, then the *Sunday Telegraph*. I could shut up my little house and go anywhere at a moment's notice. But when I came home again, it was me, the cat, and (more often than not) a bowl of ramen noodles.

Over the years I have continuously thanked Bill for rescuing me from what I call "certain spinsterhood." He thinks I'm joking. I'm not.

How do you make room for a relationship? How do you make room for a child? Every woman does it her own way. My way, my all-or-nothing way, was to ditch work completely and concentrate all my energy on my family. I gave up the cottage. The cat made the altruistic move of running away by itself. I sold my convertible and moved into the city to a large family-size apartment a block from the park. Molly was born two weeks after we moved in.

Some decisions make themselves, and some decisions aren't even decisions. You turn down one piece of work because you don't want to travel, another because you're tired, then another because your brain feels rusty—and before you know it, three years have gone by and you can list every child's activity in your neighborhood, every kids TV show, every baby food product and clothing label, and you're telling people you are thinking of writing for *Sesame Street*. You weigh about twenty pounds more than you ever imagined, and people who are put next to you at dinner parties ask you for your husband's opinions.

This became my life—and I loved it. It was cozy. I loved my baby and loved the novelty of being a mother. I loved staying in one place. I actually loved not having to think. But I had a friend once who after a few years of motherhood asked how it was possible that so much love and so much boredom could coexist in the same breast. And some days on the playground I knew exactly what she was talking about.

To offset the ennui of dealing solely with small children, some women live vicariously in their husband's world during their years at home. This is particularly easy when your husband's world is one you used to inhabit yourself. If you worked in finance and your husband is at a merchant bank, or you are both used to affecting government policy, or you were a journalist and your husband is now the managing editor of the *New York Times*, the dinnertime conversation has somewhere to go besides baby's first steps. My husband was promoted to managing editor at about the time Molly was born. We talked about news stories all the time. I didn't lose my brain, but I was losing my identity. I'm not joking when I tell you that people used to come up to me and ask me what Bill thought about X, Y or Z. Nor am I joking when I used to answer, "He thinks that . . ." before telling them what *I* thought.

Did I feel "invisible"? I felt too fat to be invisible!

When Peggy Orenstein interviewed women about their life choices in 2000 for her book *Flux,* she came to the conclusion that the women she surveyed who decided to leave the workforce when they had their children "[a]lmost universally . . . were married to men who worked long hours, earning far more money than they ever could. That allowed them the luxury of 'choosing' to quit their jobs, but it also created a situation in which they felt they had to: The demands of their husbands' jobs, which they felt were inviolable, left them solely responsible for childcare and household management. Layering those tasks over full-time work quickly became overwhelming."[1]

As far as my situation was concerned, Orenstein had it exactly right. Bill worked long hours and earned a lot more money than I could. Someone had to run the household. I did feel that the demands of his job were inviolable, but his job wasn't a burden to our lifestyle; to me it was an exciting reminder of the world I had decided to leave for the time being.

The home I was creating for our family had many similarities to the one I had grown up in. I was born and raised in London into a world where women of my background didn't attend college. Instead—even in the 1980s—they got married. The year I went to King's College London only a handful of the other girls who were leaving my convent boarding school were doing the same thing. Today, thirty years later, almost every girl who leaves the same school goes on to a place at a decent college.

I was brought up to be more now than then. My American mother, who had gone to college in New York, had met my English father while they were both working journalists in Paris. I was a dual national, and my mother never stopped telling me that I was only "half English," just as much an American as a Brit. She was trying to give me a sense of my options, but as a young child who only wanted to fit in, I hated the reminders. Anyway, she was as keen to fit in as I was. On having her children (three in all), she did as the other London mothers she knew did and stayed home in her large white house with her family, a live-in au pair, and a nanny. But this was not the world she was used to, and she was never comfortable in it. Once we were at school, she left my father and returned to journalism. She had previously been a successful feature writer for the *New York Herald-Tribune*. Now she went back to the same career at the same paper, though in her second incarnation she was a freelancer, fitting in her pieces around her family. She still got quality assignments, though. I remember her trying to explain to us in the late 1960s why interviewing the Beatles was exciting.

Unlike my mother, I had never thought I would stop working when I had children. My career had been so consuming and such a part of my identity I didn't think I could exist without it. Well, that's not entirely true. I knew I could exist without it; I just didn't know who I would be.

The effect that staying at home has on a marriage really depends on your confidence. Everything about staying at home depends on your confidence, as you will see throughout this book. The biggest adjustment women face when they give up work—more even than losing an income—is that their confidence starts to decline. Being in the outside world, getting paid, and communicating with adults is healthy and energizing. Giving that up is tough on an ego. Some women feel diminished and inadequate. Some get lonely and depressed. They can be very, very busy and very, very bored. They can become hard to live with.

I'll give you my own example. Before I stayed at home I had been confident enough to move from country to country, go out on my own, basically do whatever I wanted to do. After I'd been home full-time for a few months, I rarely went out socially in New York without Bill. It became harder and harder to walk into a room by myself. If we were invited to something as a couple and Bill couldn't make it, I didn't go. Having people ask me for Bill's opinions rather than my own definitely had something to do with it. I only started accepting invitations by myself once I was working on this book, and the first few times that I told people Bill couldn't come, I apologized for being "just me."

During this period of my life I never thought about what would happen in the future, just as I had never thought about getting married and having children—or even having a boyfriend—while I was writing my Winnie Mandela book. I lived entirely in the present. If you had asked me when I was a new mother what I thought I would be doing in ten years' time, I would have stared at you blankly. It never occurred to me that there was an end to this period. I wonder now, if I had known that I was merely at home for a few years, whether I would have been able to remain a more confident woman. There's no question that staying at home made me a more confident mother. Why, then, did I feel like such a wimp out in the world?

When Molly was two I became pregnant again, but we lost the baby late in the pregnancy. The following year I turned forty, Bill became a columnist at the *New York Times*, and I began to think about going back to work. Yet I didn't think of going back to the professional life I had had before. Instead I did a few things that fit in with my family. I did some—but not many—freelance pieces for magazines, newspapers, and Web sites. These were brief little pieces, tiny sound bites of writing that took no time at all. I'd write paragraphs reviewing a restaurant or a book, or previewing a movie. Occasionally I'd fill in for a London columnist who happened to be on vacation. I also read and edited a few manuscripts for friends, and I continued to live vicariously through Bill's job, acting as his editor when he wrote.

After 9/11 I became pregnant with Alice. I remember feeling relief in knowing that having another baby meant I wouldn't be expected to work. I was beginning to wonder if I would ever work again. By now I was so lacking in professional confidence (I'd been home for five years), I couldn't imagine anyone wanting to hire me. Having Alice meant I could concentrate on my new baby and continue being a full-time mother. I would have found this a difficult choice to justify without her, as Molly was now in kindergarten and didn't need me there between the hours of 8:30 and 3:00. We no longer had any babysitting help, apart from the occasional college girl on the rare evenings when we went out. A lot of the time it was just my girls and me. And their dad. Bill was around a lot in those days, too. Writers usually are. He'd get home in the late afternoon, easily in time to tell the girls bedtime stories. He'd play with them and he'd cook for them. I look back on those years as a golden time for our family. Of course it couldn't last.

In the early summer of 2003, Bill called home from the office to say he had been asked if he was interested in being considered for the job of executive editor of the *Times*. As we discussed whether he should say yes, I pictured the future of our family. I saw a life where the phone rang incessantly, where there was little privacy and not much downtime. I imagined attention that was both fawning and critical. I could see Bill's children being the recipients of unwanted interest because of their father. I realized our home would be an oasis in the middle of all of this, precious but more difficult to preserve and protect.

On the other hand, what a great opportunity for us as parents! Imagine a childhood where the newsroom's your schoolroom. Imagine the opportunities for travel and the exciting exposure to the world and its people. If your goal as a parent is to raise children with compassionate, engaged, inquiring minds, there could be no better environment than this.

What would my role be in this new life? To the outside world I would probably become simultaneously more and less visible. Should I be feminine or a feminist? Ironically, having spent years writing about the complications of being a public or semipublic wife, I couldn't figure out how to be one myself. I knew there was a role to be played as Mrs. *New York Times* (a *role* not a job). I knew it was mine to define as I chose, but I had no idea how to do it.

I asked my predecessor and good friend Carolyn Lelyveld for advice. Carolyn also had two daughters, but they were grown by the time her husband, Joe, was made executive editor. Carolyn had been a maternal figure to many families at the paper, including ours. She spent most of her life working with children, and while Joe was editor she was a constant presence at PS 111 Adolph S. Ochs School, a local school with an affiliation with the New York Times Company Foundation. Carolyn was very sick when I talked to her and would die from complications from breast cancer within the year. Her advice was always punchy. She told me to be myself. Easy for her to say! Which self was that? I now had as many identities as Sybil.

There comes a time as the mother of daughters when you begin to see the value of yourself as their role model. Here's the conundrum: you want to be around to take care of them, and you want to be there when they need you, yet you want them to see you as an independent woman so that they grow up to be independent women, too. You don't want them to think their independence will only last until they have their own children, at which point they will retire into the care of their loving and patriarchal husbands. You are exposing them to a world where women are in positions of power, yet you are still cocooned at home. If being independent means becoming less available, what's the best thing to do?

This dilemma began percolating in my head just after Alice turned two. She had recently started in a playgroup across the street, and now even she was gone for three mornings a week. One morning we got into the elevator with the girls to go about our days when Alice looked up and said, "I go to school. Molly goes to school. Daddy goes to work. And Mommy goes to . . . gym." And that was that. Instant devastation! I was now a gym-goer. With that remark I knew it was time to move on. I could no longer be "just" a mother or "just" a wife, or just a gym-goer. I wanted to use my brain for my own interests. I had to get back out there again. It became clear that the way to make all of these identities cohesive was to haul the old professional identity out of storage, dust it off, and take it back on the road. But how?

During my last couple of years at home a number of feature stories had appeared in newspapers, magazines, and on television about the difficulties facing women who had left careers to return to work. Many of these stories were based on work done by the author Sylvia Ann Hewlett and her associates at the Center for Work-Life Policy. The CWLP focuses on improving working conditions for parents, and at about the time I was thinking about going back to work it was shining a spotlight on the needs of women like me. In my case their good intentions had a debilitating effect. The stories they generated were about off-ramps and on-ramps. As they tried to convince companies to make it easier for women to clamber back up onto an on-ramp (and they have had some valuable success in achieving this), they talked about how it was practically impossible to do so.

You know when you're pregnant and you get told about all the diseases and disabilities your baby could be born with? At some point you begin to wonder if it's possible to have a healthy child. This is how I felt as I heard about all the obstacles that stood between my next job and me. I learned that I could never make the same money as I had before, that I would have to take a demotion, that 66 percent of the "highly qualified women at home with their children" who had been interviewed by Hewlett "wanted to be back at work full-time and were finding reentry extremely difficult."

How depressing is that? What should I do? I was already feeling inadequate and insecure after seven years at home. This news didn't exactly make me feel like racing out of the house clutching my résumé.

After a while I did what you do in the face of any bad diagnosis: I chose to ignore the larger numbers and instead concentrated on the 33 percent who had been successful. This is where the reporting that turned into this book began. I looked for stories from women who had managed to reclaim a career after several years at home. At that stage my aim was solely to hear about how and what they had done and to learn from their experience. Most of the stories I had read about women returning to work were set in a corporate environment. But few of the women I know work in the business world. I wanted to broaden the base, find a variety of careers, and see what the similarities or differences might be.

A reporter's instinct when she hears an interesting story is to retell it, and that's what happened with me. I identified with the women I talked to, and I began to think about telling their stories for the benefit of other women in the same situation. At the same time, I began to find out what women had done historically. Certainly my mother's story loomed large: if she had managed to start writing again in the 1960s, the idea that you could restart a career after children couldn't be new or impossible.

I was born in 1961. In October of that year, Barnard College began a pilot program under a grant from the Carnegie Corporation to stem the "waste of talent and abilities among educated women." This was essentially a job-hunting program for married, middle-class and middle-aged women. The average attendee had married young and was the mother of several children, ranging in age from college to grade school. Money was not an issue to her; she wanted paid employment for her own self-esteem. As she prepared to reenter the job market, both her husband and her children stood behind her. "Employees are beginning to appreciate that maturity and judgment are dandy," said Anne Cronin, the director of the program, in an interview at the time. "And that stability is worth its weight in pearls."

The idea that women with school- or college-age children can be a valuable asset to the labor market isn't new now, and it wasn't particularly new then. But back then it didn't sound revolutionary for a mother who had been at home for some time to think about returning to work. In 1960 the Radcliffe Institute for Independent Study was established to help married housewives resume and progress in their professional development. (This is not to be confused with the Radcliffe Institute for Advanced Study, the remaining segment of Radcliffe College, whose dean, Drew Faust, was named first female president of Harvard University in 2007.) A *New York Times* story from February 1962 claimed, "Seven million additional women are expected to enter the labor market in the next decade, a majority of whom are in their forties." The story further noted, "Increasing numbers of educated women are seeking work after marriage and child-bearing."

In 1967 Smith College chose the theme "The Spread of My Life" for its twenty-five-year reunion, and it is an apt theme for this book. That year each member of the class of 1942 from all the Seven Sisters colleges was sent a questionnaire. Most of the women who answered it were married with children. Yet they expected to charge off in different directions during the next twenty-five years, many of them seeking further education and new careers. "We don't feel left out. We feel we have a whole new life ahead of us," said Mrs. Allen Howland of Warwick, Rhode Island, who had majored in music at college, taught it for several years before marriage and children, and at that time was looking to get a master's degree before resuming her career.

A whole slew of articles describing mature (over twenty-six years old) women returning to college to finish degrees or study for further degrees appeared in local papers across the country from the 1960s on. I was eight years old when the *Oshkosh Daily Northwestern* ran a photograph of a group of well-groomed middle-aged wives, who were studying for new degrees, on the same page as its wedding and engagement announcements.

In 1977 I turned sixteen, and Janet Copley wrote a nationally published column under the headline "Why Do Women Return to Work?" She specifically mentioned women whose children had grown. "If they didn't work," she pointed out, "they wouldn't have much to do."

In 1984, the year I began my career, a branch of the YWCA in Pittsburgh held a series of workshops for mothers with children who were planning on returning to the workforce. The advice on offer ranged from balancing family and work, examining skills to see whether new training would be appropriate, and a discussion of wardrobe needs.

You get the point. The idea that women return to work having spent several years being full-time mothers is not new and has never been impossible.

Here is a historical context for the lives you will read about in *The Comeback* so that you keep a sense of perspective for what the women in this book have accomplished. In addition to a variety of careers, I also wanted to look at a range in age and geographical locations so that you didn't feel (as one of my friends put it) that you were just reading about the women in my building. The ages of the women in *The Comeback* range from the mid-forties to the mid-sixties. They are middle-aged and middle-class. They all went to college. They all had careers—not jobs—that they gave up for their children. Under that umbrella, though, you will find a lawyer, a venture capitalist, a photographer, a teacher, a furniture designer, a human rights activist, and a doctor. Each story examines a different career but also looks at the different issues facing wives, mothers, and working women. Mothers with careers have a certain amount of choice. The women in this book were no exception. Some of the decisions they faced are universal, not unique to their particular career. For example, you might not be a furniture designer, but you might be married to a man who is now retired and wants you to quit your second career to travel with him. You might not work in finance, but you might have a child with chronic health issues. You might not be a doctor, but you might be getting divorced.

Because this book is called *The Comeback* I have often been asked whether the women who are featured in it came back to the exact jobs they left. The answer is no. They have come back to the workforce, and in one case (briefly) to the same employer, but in terms of where they resumed their work, they haven't so much come back as moved on. This is by choice. Would you want to return to the exact job you held several years ago? Aren't you a different person with different needs and interests?

However, let's think about the whole nature of coming back and success. Is it enough to say that you have successfully come back simply because you have managed to get a job? Shouldn't you be doing at least as well as you were before? The answer becomes complicated when mothers decide that they want and need different things from their work experience. If you think of life in terms of a jigsaw puzzle, when you have children suddenly there are many more pieces to fit together. More pieces get added as the family grows older. Different issues crop up once women have settled back into work the second time around. As her children become increasingly independent, a woman's parents become less so. Health problems move around inside a family. Husbands retire, and with time on their hands they look for companionship that might no longer be available. Money is an issue, too, of course. Not only the affluent take advantage of the choice to stay at home. In more than one case in this book, the wife outearned her husband before she quit and after she returned. Those salaries are vital to the financial health of a family. What sacrifices are made in the pursuit of these choices?

You already know how insecure I felt facing my own comeback. Insecurity is an isolating experience—everyone else seems so much more capable of taking on the world than you. But as I found out, there was nothing new or unusual here, either. In 1973 Caroline Bird wrote *Everything a Woman Needs to Know to Get Paid What She's*

Worth, which she updated a few years later in a version called *Everything a Woman Needs to Know to Get Paid What She's Worth . . . in the 1980s*. In her book she answered questions such as "I want to stop working for a few years until my children are older. What can I do to be sure I can get back in?" "How do you hunt for a job the second time around?" and "Can you ever go back to the job you would have had if you had never stopped working?"[2]

As she sensibly pointed out, there are many ways to ease back into a career. Some women reeducate themselves into reentry. Others try for part-time jobs. Some get paid work as a logical development of their volunteerism. Bird made a point of mentioning volunteer work, because "Volunteer work builds confidence in itself." She described the industry of consultants, workshops, manuals, and counselors ready to help women identify the value of their non-job experiences to employers. That same industry thrives today, particularly on the Internet, where women are encouraged to sign up with networking organizations that will (for a fee) shape a résumé or post a job opening. Bird felt the same way as I do, which is, if you think you need help of this kind, then go ahead and take it. "The principal value of this advice, as its purveyors are the first to admit, is to build a woman's confidence. If she thinks she needs it. She probably does."

Cynthia Leivie, the editor of *Glamour*, once pointed out that women don't want to have it all, they want to *do* it all, and I think she is closer to the mark of what drives us. From the vantage point of sitting and writing this introduction two years after Alice defined me as a gym-going mother, I think it is possible to do it all, or have it all, if you want to. Just not over the course of one working day or a week. Start to think in terms of your whole life. Here you are in your twenties, energetic and a dedicated careerist, working hard and probably traveling for your job. Now you are a mother with babies and small children. If you want to stay at home and take care of them full-time (and not every mother does), then do it. It doesn't mean you will never get another job. It's a finite stage.

Eventually those children will start kindergarten and you'll have some hours to yourself during the day. Perhaps you'll volunteer with those hours or find part-time work. You won't want to disappear completely as a mother. Children still come home from school, want help with homework, and have games and practices that they have to get to. Their needs change, but they don't disappear. They'll still cry and need to be comforted. They'll want your praise. They'll look for your answers to their questions. During this period of your life, you'll need some flexibility. You won't be alone.

Today nearly 30 percent of the entire workforce in the United States (both male and female) have a flexible work schedule that allows them to vary the time they begin or end work, according to the latest study released by the Bureau of Labor Statistics. A breakdown of the study shows that flexible schedules are most common among what the bureau calls "management, business and related occupations"—that is, career workers.

A desire for flexibility has always led many women to try to work part-time. Some of the women in this book eased back into work on a part-time basis either by working shorter working weeks or by taking temporary projects. Others are looking to ease back down to part-time from full-time as they get older. These days a shortened schedule is a definite choice. But there are pros and cons, and you should remember that the cons can be hefty. As other books have shown, most notably Arlie Hochschild's *The Second Shift,* women who work still have primary responsibility for both child and home care.[3] Somewhere lies a balance between having too much time and too much to do. The idea—or maybe the *ideal*—of working part-time is that you have enough time during the day or the week to do it all.

In order to chase that ideal you should be able to define what part-time is. What's your definition? Actually, what's your definition of full-time? Are you still thinking in terms of the traditional forty-hour week spread from 9:00 to 5:00 over five days? I bet if you are working full-time in a competitive career, you're working longer hours and possibly more days than that. In December 2006 an article titled "Extreme Jobs: The Dangerous Allure of the 70-Hour Work-week" ran in the *Harvard Business Review*, and the title alone tells you everything you need to know.[4] One of the women profiled in this book considered asking her employers if she could go to a "reduced schedule" of leaving the office at 5:00 instead of 7:00 p.m. This at the end of a day that begins at about 8:30 in the morning.

Even in Europe, where countries like France have strictly regulated hours and the thirty-five-hour basic week remains the standard, many employees work well in excess of forty hours a week. The U.S. government doesn't define full-time, believing it to be a matter for individual employers. But at the Bureau of Labor Statistics, where some kind of breakdown has to exist, workers are classified as full-time if they work thirty-five hours or more in a week; part-time if they work up to thirty-four. If that's the case, what qualifies for part-time work can actually be more like full-time work for part-time pay—with little or no benefits.

While part-time and what is now commonly referred to as "flex-time" both have their own elastic definitions ranging from a day or two less a week, to an hour or two less a day, to working a few intensive months a year and then being at home full-time, one aspect of this kind of employment is pretty constant: the compensation isn't as good. If you work full-time, you are four times more likely to get health insurance than if you work part-time and three times as likely to be given some kind of a retirement package.[5]

I know from my own experience—and from the experiences of the women in this book—how hard it can be to be your own advocate, especially when you are coming back to work after a long time away. Mothers who have accomplished the impossible in finding places to live, or getting their children the right medical care or into a decent school, have faltered as they described their own negotiations about pay or benefits. The tone and substance of their conversation was admirably powerful when they talked about what they did on behalf of their families. Yet they sounded insecure and uncertain as they considered their own professional prospects.

I didn't end up getting a job as such, I ended up with the assignment that is this book. I worked for several months on spec (without pay) putting together a proposal that I eventually felt confident enough to show to agents and publishers. As the proposal took shape, my confidence grew. I noticed that as I became more confident, I relaxed more as a wife and mother. Previously I had felt I had to be there for the girls, come what may. Now I don't feel guilty if Bill takes the kids to school instead of me. And since I've had my own projects to work on, I don't spend much time thinking about how to be Mrs. *New York Times*. I go to events I am interested in (even without Bill!) and don't show up to those I don't care about. Contrary to what my friends may believe, I don't edit the paper each day. But I feel comfortable in telling my husband my opinions as well as acting as his sounding board. I have finally found a way of taking Carolyn's advice and becoming myself.

Once you have children, you will never go back to the old way of doing things, but I have found that I've been able to regain more of my old life than I'd thought possible. I'd been freelancing for a long time before I became a mother, so I was used to setting my own hours. I've always worked hardest and fastest in the first part of the day. That kind of rhythm has meant that I've been able to leave my work and pick up my children from school without any guilt. I always liked to travel for a story and I still do. The brief trips to see the women profiled here (usually about two days at a time) have been welcome breaks from my family routine. And it's been nice to tell my daughters that I'm going to work as I pack a suitcase, not a gym bag.

It is so hard to give someone confidence. When Harvard president Drew Faust was a girl, her mother constantly told her, "It's a man's world, sweetie, and the sooner you learn that, the better off you'll be." Change just one tiny part of that sentence and it becomes an empowering mantra for a comeback: "It's *your* world, sweetie, and the sooner you learn that, the better off you'll be."

Judith Feder

You tell me who has to leave the office when the kid bumps
his head on a radiator or slips on a milk carton.
Wendy Wasserstein, *Isn't It Romantic* (1983)

MEET THE FEDERS. They could be the twenty-first-century Manhattan family of your dreams. Dad, Warren, is an investment banker. Every day you can see him walk from his Upper East Side co-op apartment to his Midtown office—right after he has cooked breakfast for the family and seen the twins off to school. Mom, Judith, a vice president at a venture capital company is described as "very, very pretty" by one of her daughters. With her long, thick brown hair hanging down her back and that sparkle in her large brown eyes, she looks much younger than her fifty-four years. She's the glue that holds this family together. She knows where everyone's meant to be at any given moment, and will drop everything to get them there if she needs to.

Beautiful older daughter, Julianne, is up at Williams College, where she gets straight A's. The teenage twins, Katie and Robbie, are both at prestigious New York City private schools. Robbie just failed to get on the tennis team by *this much*. He's really disappointed, but he'll still play—and jog and fence. When he's not doing homework, he likes to read history books, and he'd rather chat with you than with your kids. Katie's the captain of the cross-country team and works in a mentoring program, coaching some of the city's more disadvantaged kids in basketball. And maybe at some point the family will all manage to get together out at their beach house in Amagansett, Long Island. Here, they are a group, because that's how they like to be—together, not separate. They're one another's best friends; they all tell you that. Apart from the summertime, when they tend to head their own ways, they still arrange to vacation collectively. The Caribbean at Christmas, Hawaii for spring break. There, you'll see them out on the tennis courts playing against one another in the early morning; later they'll be snorkeling and swimming; they might have massages or trainers (booked by Judith); and in the evening, if they're not eating out at a restaurant (prebooked by Judith from New York), they'll enjoy a gourmet meal whipped up by Julianne, who loves to cook.

This is what you would see if you met the Feders today. A wonderful, blooming, affluent, happy family. Not a problem in sight. Mom's job could be a little more challenging, but she doesn't want the demands that might go with more excitement. She likes to be able to get out of the office on time, or even a little early to catch one of the kids' games. She has less energy than when she was younger, even if she seems buzzing with vitality.

Now let's roll the clock back.

There is nothing like a sick child to bring a mother to a screeching halt. Annual checkups have been reassuringly named "well-child visits" for a reason. The best trips to the doctor are those when you're told that it's only a virus, everyone has it, there's nothing to be done, just wait it out. You've spent your twenty dollars co-payment or your uninsured one hundred dollars for a pointless diagnosis, but it's been money well spent. The rash, the choking cough, or the high temperature are all "normal." You can go about your day. You stop in at the pharmacy for some over-the-counter medicine, throw in a coloring book or a cheap plastic toy, and you're done. You can even go back to work with a clear conscience. But what if it's not just a virus? What if your child is so sick, or is sick for so long, that you have to stay at home?

Not all decisions about staying at home are easy. Not all mothers who stay with their children choose to because they want to inhabit a cozy world of playgroups and playgrounds. And the only hard choice about quitting work doesn't have to be one involving money. You can have the best career in the world and be able to afford top-quality help, but your child may have problem after problem. Your child may really need you at home.

This is a story about those problems. So much goes wrong during the first part of this story that it's hard to believe anyone ends up actually surviving it, let alone flourishing. But what you should know about Judith Feder from the start is that she is a fighter. She's actually more than that.

Judith has long been something of a legend in her own family. She is more than up to handling a challenge, and she's one of those wives and mothers whose energy and enthusiasm galvanize her husband and three kids on a daily basis. "It's never dull with her. You can say that for sure," said Katie. They're proud of her feisty, larger-than-life personality even as they point out, "With my mom you can lose the fight even though she can be wrong." They take pride in listing what she's accomplished for them. And what she has done includes leaving her career and staying home for ten years as she took care of them all when they needed her most.

The Feders all talk about how as a mother Judith combines strength and gentleness, qualities that are obvious when you meet her. She is very tough, very direct, but cheerful and kind. You can imagine her just as easily at a corporate meeting or a parent-teacher conference. She comes across as an attractive, strong working mother. It was with that strength and confidence that she went in for an ultrasound and amniocentesis test in the second trimester of her second pregnancy, back in 1991, and announced to the nurse unequivocally that the only thing she wanted was "not twins!"

She already had a little girl, Julianne, who at three years old was a dream child. She didn't mind whether her second child would be a son or a second daughter, and it went without saying that she wanted a healthy baby. She hoped that her second experience would be as easy and as uncomplicated as her first.

Her first pregnancy was one that many of us can only dream about. A little sickness, not too much; little weight gain, not too much. Not tired, but blooming and easily able to spend nine months of going about her day, working her usual long hours at her investment job. Back then she was financing her own real estate development deals all over the country. In the decade since she had graduated from Tufts University, then Hofstra Law School, she had progressed from being a lawyer in the general counsel's office of Merrill Lynch's real estate group, to working for a large real estate development firm, to working for herself, making more money with each step. By the time she became pregnant, she specialized in financing developments in what she called "unappealing areas," in deals that were generally considered to be small—$1 million to $10 million.

It was 1988. She and her husband, Warren, had been married for three years. They had met when they were set up by Warren's mother, who had met Judith at a family wedding and in the tradition of mothers all over the world had urged her son to ask her out. Warren was a smart, mild-mannered, well-educated lawyer from New York, who had recently returned to the city from the London office of a New York law firm. Eventually he took his mother's advice and made the call. They chatted for a while, as Judith, whose bark is far worse than her bite, told him that he seemed very socially awkward.

She had "enormous reservations" about going out with him, she later said, though she wasn't exactly clear why. In the end she agreed to give it a try, and they booked a Sunday brunch together. And that was it. The brunch lasted five or six hours. By the third date they were seeing each other exclusively. It's a romantic story, one of instant attraction, but it also tells you a lot about the kind of people Warren and Judith are. In many ways they are alike. They know their own minds. They make decisions easily, and they stick with them. They are loyal and tenacious.

The late eighties were the heyday of the yuppie couple, and Warren and Judith fit right in. Here's a brief reminder of the stereotype from *The 1980s: The Way We Lived*.[1]

Many of the middle-class young who came out of college in the late 1970s and early 1980s went into well-paid jobs in finance, the media, law, and property development. In the economic turmoil of the early Reagan presidency (1981–89), anyone who was young and ambitious could make a lot of money and make it fast. They became known as yuppies, which stood for young urban professionals. Their motto for life was "Whoever dies with the most toys wins."

Obsessed with their careers and their collections of gadgets, yuppies delayed marriage and children . . . As more and more women went into well-paid jobs, yuppie couples found themselves with a lot of money and plenty of ways to spend it. Childless yuppie couples became known as "dinks" or "dinkys," because they had "dual incomes and no kids (yet)." Those with children hired nannies, housekeepers, and other servants so they could keep up with their careers and partying lifestyle. Putting a child through the "right" school became as important as taking holidays in the "right" resorts.

The Feders both loved their jobs and worked hard; two incomes were coming home, so there was plenty of money. Less in the fridge, though—maybe club soda, orange juice, coffee, and water was all there'd be most of the time. They ordered in meals, ate out, took nice vacations, spent summers in Amagansett, played tennis. Their life was settled and easy.

Becoming parents had been easy, too. They talked about it and, as Warren said, "The next day she was pregnant." There had been little for Judith to organize domestically before the baby was born. She didn't have to move to a bigger house—they'd already done that, having previously bought a family-sized co-op apartment on East Sixty-fourth Street. Never much of a shopper, Judith was fortunate that her sister Bonnie had had her second baby nine months earlier and could part with plenty of hand-me-downs.

With the domestic end taken care of, Judith was able to work right up until the last minute, and when her labor began she headed to the hospital. The delivery was a natural childbirth with no drugs. Not by choice. Judith had been adamant that she wanted an epidural. But the whole thing was so short, so *easy*—only three and a half hours from start to finish—that there just wasn't time for pain relief. There wasn't time for anything, really. Judith had been in the middle of closing a deal when her labor started, and one of the lawyers involved called back to finalize details forty-five minutes after the delivery. When Warren came back into the room, an hour after Julianne's birth, he found that not only was Judith up, but she had also already moved the furniture around and was busy on the phone. Was she *already* back at work or *still* at work? Did it matter? She felt fine, the baby was fine. The phone call wasn't a distraction. She was thirty-four years old.

She didn't take a maternity leave, but got up and returned to her office as soon as Julianne was organized at home. Partly this was because she had a good support system. She had family; Bonnie, who was fifteen months older and lived a few blocks away, already had her two boys, age two and nine months. Being involved with Bonnie's kids before having her own meant that Judith knew how to get started. She knew what Julianne needed, and if she had any questions or problems, she could call her sister. And she had full-time live-in help.

She got her first nanny through a woman who found work for women from the Philippines, charging prospective employers a small fee for making the introductions. "My sister and I were hooked into that network, and there were tons of young girls looking for work, so we just happened to hire two at the same time—they didn't know each other before." The two sisters made sure that their nannies were compatible and could overlap schedules where necessary. Eventually the cousins would go to the same schools.

There was another reason Judith felt able—or maybe it's more accurate to say she felt the need—to go back to work so quickly: she was her own boss. She had to run her company. The benefit of this was that to a large extent she could dictate her own schedule. There were heavy demands on her time, and she traveled, but she could come home unexpectedly, and she had arranged her life so that her office was in walking distance from her apartment. When you are trying to combine work and family life, it really helps to cut out the commute.

At this point she was earning as much as Warren, with the potential to out-earn him in a good year. Warren had left his own job at a Wall Street law firm to concentrate on running his family business of manufacturing hairbrushes. His work involved a fair amount of travel, too, but his was to suppliers in the Far East and was for longer periods of time. Over the course of a year he'd be gone for as much as two or three months, broken into trips that would last two or three weeks at a time.

Despite the pressures of work, the Feders wanted to have more children and started trying soon after Julianne was born. Judith was conscious of age-related fertility issues, but with Warren out of town so much it wasn't easy to get pregnant. Meanwhile, Julianne was such a good-natured child, "everyone wanted to take care of her." The family could and did still eat out; they would take Julianne along with them to restaurants. Having one child was easy, especially one as sunny as theirs.

It took three and a half years for Judith to get pregnant again. By the time she did, she was thirty-seven—not the oldest expectant mother you've heard of, but not that young, either. When she went into the hospital in 1991 to have an amniocentesis test at eighteen weeks, she had her first sonogram. Unusually, she hadn't had one earlier, but she hadn't thought anything of it. If the first pregnancy was any guide, she had nothing to worry about. It was during the course of this comparatively late first sonogram that the nurse discovered Judith was expecting twins. No one (including her ob-gyn) had suspected anything like this. Judith was so shaken that she started screaming in the exam room. Warren was ecstatic, although his excitement was slightly tempered when on his way out he was stopped and asked to pay an additional twelve hundred dollars—the charge for the second amnio procedure.

That twelve hundred dollars was like an entry fee into a new, much more difficult world. "I was so unprepared, I was working, I didn't have the room, the apartment wasn't big enough, I just wasn't ready to manage the situation," said Judith, describing all of her reactions at once.

Now it was a tough pregnancy. Suddenly problems popped up everywhere. In a number of these stories you'll see that ill health and death of parents often run concurrently with major incidences of birth or career changes. Judith's story is a case in point. Her mother, to whom she was very close, had had a bout of breast cancer when Judith was in college. Since then she had been in remission. A burst of pain when she was playing with her grandsons in the park led to the news that the cancer was back and had spread to her bones. At the same time that Judith found out about the twins, she was already coping with the fact that her mother didn't have long to live.

Judith moved her prenatal care to Cornell Medical Center, where the doctors had more experience with multiple births. Older mothers giving birth to multiples was a growing phenomenon in New York. According to the National Center for Health Statistics, the twin birthrate has risen 55 percent since 1980, and is currently 29.3 per 1,000 live births. The rise in multiple births could partly be attributed to an increase in fertility treatments, which Judith hadn't had. But she was an older mother, and older mothers are more likely to have twins.

Her condition was now more precarious. She had to wear a monitor and check the two heartbeats twice a day. She was at high risk for preterm labor, which would bring its own list of dangers. At twenty-six weeks she went to the hospital because she was leaking amniotic fluid. A few hours later, when the leaking stopped, she was sent home. She was never put on bed rest, nor was she told to take any special precautions. Eventually she put herself to bed. But on December 10, 1991, at twenty-eight weeks, after their blood pressure and heart rates dropped, her twins were born by emergency C-section.

Everything about this birth was different from Julianne's. The only similarity was the speed. The twins were born quickly, but the experience was noisy and frightening. There were at least fifteen people in the operating room participating in an alarming surgery three months before its time. At two pounds three ounces (Katie) and two pounds six ounces (Robbie), the twins weighed less than chickens at the supermarket, a fact their mother liked to point out to them throughout their childhood. They were immediately taken to the neonatal intensive care unit (NICU), where they were quickly hooked up to monitors and breathing apparatus. The family was so unprepared for this series of events that they hadn't even thought about what to call their twins. In the end Julianne named them, after a Robbie and a Katie that she already knew from summer camp.

Judith spent five days in the hospital recovering from the surgery. There was little rest, though. While her premature newborns were in the NICU, her mother was having cancer treatment in the same hospital, wracked with pain and on morphine. Nobody could have imagined the life Judith was suddenly leading. It was, as Warren later described it, "beyond doubt, the roughest period of our life." On one floor Judith's mother was dying. On another her babies were fighting for their lives—tiny, undernourished, and unwell. They were too small to eat properly and needed constant monitoring, especially at night (sleep apnea is very common in preemies). She had a four-year-old daughter who needed her. Her husband tried to be available, but he was preoccupied with his own family. The hair products business that his family owned and ran was suffering. There were both personnel and financial problems, and if the company was to avoid falling into bankruptcy, it had to be pulled into good enough shape to be sold. Warren had to be on the road for four days a week meeting with employees and clients. Meanwhile, Judith couldn't help but ignore her own clients. She was worried, extremely depressed, and exhausted.

You can see that this is not the type of decision we normally talk about in a conversation about whether or not women might stay at home with their children or go back to work. Here is a woman who was in the midst of a crisis and who reacted instinctively. Everything about the situation she faced was impossibly hard. Yet ironically this meant her decision to stop work was easy. There was no choice.

After one client tried to reach her without success for three weeks, Judith realized that she couldn't continue working. Something had to give. Her decision might have made itself, but that didn't mean she was happy with it. But then she wasn't happy at all. "I cried all the time," she said. "I was so depressed. I was beside myself all the time."

Of the two twins, Katie had fewer problems. She had some blood issues and she wasn't making bile, but her problems resolved themselves and she was able to come home in six weeks. Robbie had much more to cope with. A rash on his face turned out to be a staph infection that spread like wildfire through his tiny body, nearly killing him. (Staphylococcus is a group of bacteria that causes a rash on the skin. It can, however, become widespread when it infects the blood, which then carries the bacteria to the organs. This kind of complication is most common in people with suppressed immune systems, like people who are already in the hospital or preemies.)

The staph infection was followed by a swelling in Robbie's skull that was caused by hydrocephalus (fluid, possibly blood, pooling on his brain). Again, this was not an uncommon problem for a preemie with an immature central nervous system. But that's not to say it was normal. The treatment for this condition was—and still is—to insert a tube known as a shunt into the brain, which would drain the fluid down into the stomach so it could be absorbed as part of the circulatory process. Hydrocephalus meant the Feders had to be extra prepared that Robbie might have long-term cognitive and or physical problems.

"Every day there was something," remembered Judith, who had become a tenacious, almost vigilante-like parent in the NICU. On more than one occasion the nursing staff threatened to call security to calm her down or remove her. "My wife's true profession in life," said Warren, "and I am trying to figure out how to make this into a money-making enterprise, is to be an advocate for someone in hospital. She'll kill. She'll take no prisoners."

Robbie's shunt was inserted during one operation and then reinserted in another operation, at which point he was transferred to a different hospital. Three months after he was born he finally came home.

Warren was trying to wind down his family's hair products business and find a buyer for it. Part of this process now seems insane in retrospect, given his children's circumstances. As a cost-cutting measure, the company closed its New York office and based itself solely in Baltimore, Maryland. Warren would leave home in New York on Monday morning and not return till Thursday night. In his absence, Judith was alone, though she did have help with the three children. Every decision was hers to make, and as she was now in an unfamiliar world, she turned to her sister, whom she described as her "beacon of lucidity" through all of this, for support. Bonnie was a speech therapist and was plugged in to the special needs community that Judith needed to navigate in order to find the right help for the babies.

She had a full-time baby nurse who specialized in twins, paid for by her insurance company, for the first six weeks they were at home. Her housekeeper helped with Julianne and took care of the cleaning, shopping, and preparing meals. In the early days this level of help meant Judith could go to her office to close down her own business and visit her mother, who was now back in her apartment in the last days of her life. She died when the twins were a few months old.

After her mother died and Judith shut down her business, she devoted herself to finding the best care for Robbie and Katie. Julianne was at preschool for part of the day and had her own routine. At home she continued to be a sunny and undemanding child, who was entranced by the babies. The pressure was easing up for Judith; she was torn in fewer directions, and therefore less stressed, but life was still tough. On a typical day she would get up and feed the twins and make sure they had what they needed. "I didn't have a normal 'at home' with the kids—they were my new job."

For a few months she had to spend time dealing with her mother's estate. Her mother had left a complicated state of affairs—property rather than liquid assets; in a partnership rather than to an individual; out of state. Judith took over the disposition of the assets. She would attend to them for a brief period in the mornings by phone and fax before heading outside with her babies. She never went out with them alone. These were still babies with problems, and too many things might go wrong. As a result, outings were never relaxed affairs, but always "more of an ordeal."

Most days there was therapy. From the time they came home, the twins had the best intervention Judith and her sister could find. They saw occupational therapists, physical therapists, then speech therapists and psychologists. Initially the babies were enrolled in a program that provided therapists (paid for by the state) to come to the apartment five days a week to work with them. Then the sisters found out about a doctor who specialized in learning and developmental disorders in small children. The fact that Dr. Stanley Greenspan lived in Washington, D.C., made no difference. Judith made an appointment for him to see the twins, and then every six to nine months she would load up her minivan with them, big sister Julianne, a babysitter, two strollers, two infant carriers diapers, food, and toys and drive down to Washington for a four-hour session.

Dr. Greenspan would spend an hour with Warren, who drove in from Baltimore, and Judith, then an hour with each child individually, then another hour with Warren and Judith. He gave them suggestions for strategies, games, therapy, and supplemental help. He also predicted with an uncanny accuracy what the educational future would be like for each child. He did this when they were nine months old. Katie, he said, would be more of an even student. She had some gross motor problems, but she would overcome them and do well. She would be able to learn in the traditional way. Robbie would have some learning issues. He would be very uneven. But creatively he would be a star. He would be very bright.[2]

In the early 1990s much of the therapy for premature children with developmental problems was experimental. Being well connected and in the city—or in a part of the country—where most of the cutting-edge therapy was taking place was a great benefit to the Feders. The twins' programs were almost completely taken care of by state financing. This enormous amount of financial help meant that money was not an issue while Judith stayed home. The family was comfortably off and could afford for Judith to devote herself to her children. This might be hard to imagine, but because of the twins' condition, the Feders were actually spending *less* money than they might have. Granted, they had two babysitters for the twins the first year at home. But when Julianne started full-time kindergarten, they went down to one.

They didn't travel, apart from the road trips to D.C., where they would spend the night on the floor of Warren's nearby Baltimore apartment. They had no social life. Warren wasn't home and Judith didn't want to go out. On one occasion her sister invited her to a charity fashion show and she left early. She felt uncomfortable and out of place among women with normal lives and families.

She was living a very busy life with lots of contact with other people, but at the same time she was extremely isolated. Dealing with poor health—yours or that of your loved ones—often makes for a lonely life. Studies have shown that parents of children with health issues are more likely to end up with poor health of their own. Yet research has also shown that sick kids do much better when their own parents take care of them.[3] Warren had the pressure of his own business to distract him. Judith did not. She knew she was doing the right thing, and couldn't imagine doing anything else under the circumstances. But she had to go through her own period of mourning. She had to mourn the loss of her mother. And she had to mourn the loss of her former life. She was no longer able to bounce back, rearrange the furniture, and get back on the phone. Family progress was now measured incrementally, not in leaps or bounds. She had to change her goals. She lived in the same apartment, in the same building, in the same neighborhood. But everything about her life was different.

Although Dr. Greenspan had confidently diagnosed the twins' needs and abilities at a very young age, it wasn't clear what individual problems they might have. No developmental milestone could be taken for granted. So there was a constant worry that they might not get to the next stage. "I would say to myself, 'I want the kids to walk,' and both of them walked," said Judith. "Then they talked. They did everything late. But they were adorable. Katie had her own sense of self. She was very willful and determined. Robbie was very user friendly. He was yummy—cute and sweet—and he tried hard."

They had begun to see the well-known occupational therapist Patricia Wilbarger, who flew in from California with a new theory of sensory integration by brushing children all over their skin with a special brush to stimulate the central nervous system. Wilbarger believes that certain kinds of tactile therapies improve focus, concentration, speech, and motor skills. Her rationale is that the skin is the body's largest sensory organ—the conduit between the body's environment and the brain. Acting on the skin helps the brain process information from the environment.

They also saw a child psychiatrist, whose therapy helped them with any issues they might have from being so intensely, medically prodded and probed.

Slowly the combination of intensive therapies began to have an effect. Judith began to take the twins to regular Mommy and Me classes. Her goal from the start was for them to have lives that were integrated into the mainstream. As the children improved, her depression lifted. She described herself as being in "attack mode," with her main weapon being her own persuasive charm. She charmed her way into getting the best of everything for the twins, and it paid off.

By now you may be wondering what kind of toll being at home like this put on Judith's marriage. This was not a mother who quit her job to experience some cozy domestic heaven. Nor was this a woman with time on her hands. In less than one year the marriage had been asked to sustain the shock of the children's birth followed by the stress of not knowing how bad their health might be. It had experienced the fear of Robbie's surgeries while grieving at the death of not only Judith's mother but also the death of her father. All of this while Warren was living part-time in another city and making frequent lengthy trips to the Far East trying to save the family business where his largest customer had filed for bankruptcy.

Some marriages would have snapped under the strain. This one grew stronger. They drew strength from each other. As Warren put it, "The best of her comes out when she has to fight. I say she's a pain in the ass when things are good. But there's no better partner when things aren't." Of the two, Warren was the more optimistic, positive person. He was the glass-half-full kind of guy. Judith was the more realistic. She knew all the statistics about preemies and their prognoses. Warren thought the twins would be 100 percent of what they could be, and that would be great. He always believed in the best possible outcome. The couple was well matched, not just in terms of their outlooks but also in terms of their needs. He needed her to fight, and she needed him to make her feel better about what she was fighting for.

Eventually Warren managed to get his family business into good enough shape to sell. But it was Judith who, while socializing at a spa, found the key person who would help put together this delicate, financial transaction. Having sold the business. Warren went to work at a "regular" job, establishing a New York office for the Boston asset management firm of Gordon Brothers.

From the earliest days of their marriage, Warren and Judith had kept separate bank accounts and credit cards. They divided the bill payments between them. Warren took care of the mortgage and in-surance payments; Judith paid for all the household expenses. They continued to do this now, even though Judith wasn't working. She paid her bills from money she had saved when she was working. Pay-ing her own way while she wasn't working was of the utmost impor-tance to Judith. "I don't know what I would have done. I think I would go out of my mind if I didn't. I never want to have to ask any-one for anything," she said. "I always made my own money. I can't imagine what it would be like for a woman to buy a pocketbook and not be able to pay for it herself. I have my own checking account and he never looks at it." She paid for the housekeeper, the food, the clothes, the programs, and the school fees. When they sold her mother's Palm Beach apartment after her death, they used the money to put a down payment on a house in Amagansett. Warren took on that mortgage as well the mortgage in the city.

Part of establishing a New York office for Gordon Brothers involved finding office space. In her spare time Judith found Warren's office, negotiated the lease, ran the construction project, chose the phone system, installed Internet lines, and ordered the stationery. During the three or four months that the office took to get ready, she was there every day.

When Warren went to conferences or to weekend or networking events, she went with him, leaving the kids with the nanny. Networking was easy for her but harder for him, as he was much more reserved. So she made a point of trying to help him make contacts as an "unpaid and uncredited" partner. Some of the contacts he made were people she had done business with and known for twenty years. She now saw herself as part of her husband's career. "I think that with a lot of the men who are successful, the wives really work very, very hard at their husband's success behind the scenes. I introduced him to a bunch of people that I knew. And I kind of started him off on the right foot. But you know if he wasn't great at what he did, it wouldn't have worked. But I did make the introductions to two of the clients that he actually closed deals with, and those clients introduced him to a whole group of other clients. The circle keeps widening. I think a woman's help is invaluable to her husband."

Her help wasn't confined to Warren. She had become a walking Rolodex. People constantly called her needing to know the names of doctors, schools, fund-raisers, or investors. She had become invaluable to her community.

Her twins were slowly continuing to make their way into the mainstream. Katie went from a specialized preschool to kindergarten at the Horace Mann School, where Julianne was already enrolled and where Bonnie ran the PTA. Anyone who knows New York City private schools will have a sense of what an achievement this was. Horace Mann had one of the toughest academic programs in the city. Katie going there was both a sign of how far she had come and a display of her parents' faith in her future. Being at home with her children during these years meant that Judith constantly raised her own expectations for them. Because she expected more, they did, too. No one in this family ever settled for second best.

Robbie moved to a small, specialized kindergarten, where he began to become the student Dr. Greenberg had described—creative and idiosyncratic with some real learning issues. His fine motor skills were poor—they still are. Even today in junior high he is allowed to draw circles in his art class rather than faces, because he can't draw well. "I have terrible fine motor skills," he acknowledged cheerfully when the two of us shared a lunch in a sushi restaurant of his choosing, while he dexterously ate the contents of a bento box with chopsticks. And yet by middle school even he was doing well enough to transfer to the Allen-Stevenson School, another highly regarded Manhattan private school.

Warren was now a banker, running his own investment group within a larger merchant bank. Judith had been a full-time mother for ten years. Her life now resembled that of any comfortably off New York mother. She spent her days ferrying her three children around the city to their activities, and she networked on her husband's behalf. She volunteered and fund-raised at her kids' schools. But the fact was they were all doing fine on their own. Now that the larger pieces of her family's life were in place, all she had to attend to were the details. As a result, she was beginning to see herself more as unpaid help than an invaluable resource. Doing the grocery shopping and picking up the dirty clothes from the floor didn't exactly fill her with a sense of pride. She was getting irritable. She needed more.

An instinctive networker instinctively hooks up with a fellow expert to figure out how to make her comeback. Judith's friend Jeff Meshel believed so deeply in the concept of connections that he had written a book on the subject, *One Phone Call Away: Secrets of a Master Networker* ("Don't ask what's in it for me?" Instead, ask, "How can I help you?").[4] Meshel invited Judith to come and work part-time at his real estate investment firm, doing the same kind of work she had been so successful at in her youth.

Like many women who return to work after a prolonged absence, Judith wanted to try something new. She was keen to leave the world of financing real estate and move toward backing entrepreneurs. What she did every day wouldn't change that much, but the people she did it for would be different. While working with Meshel, Judith met one of the managing directors of a small venture capital firm that prided itself in finding the next best thing in ideas. People came to the firm for help in raising money for businesses that were developing anything from groundbreaking AIDS drugs to cutting-edge Internet use.

Judith negotiated a six-month deal for a base salary and a small percentage of her group's commission. Like many women she found negotiating on her own behalf very difficult. She felt that she couldn't drive a hard bargain. After a spectacular first few months, when she had brought in more business and raised more money than she had thought possible, she believed she could renegotiate her package. She was wrong. The six months expired and then dragged into a month-to-month situation that made her increasingly unhappy. Her attempts to improve her financial compensation were rebuffed, and eventually she learned from others at the company that her package was unlikely to improve.

Could she have done better for herself at the outset? It's hard to second-guess. She was keen to get a foot in the door; she had little relevant experience and less confidence. She might have *seemed* confident to those around her, but she felt nervous and inadequate to be restarting. She had both performance and image anxiety. She was forty-eight when she joined the firm, and she worried that her age would put her at a disadvantage.

When she looks back now, she's sure she could have done much better. Maybe she could have insisted on a mandated review of her package after six months. She could have tried to stipulate that if she reached certain goals within that time frame her compensation would improve. That way she would have had a real incentive to do well rather than just the psychological incentive of proving herself.

Judith began her reentry just when the national debate about women and work was reaching its peak. Most newspaper headlines were a variation on this one from the *Wall Street Journal*: "Mothers Who Take Time Off Must Play Career Catch-Up."[5] Business schools at Wharton, Dartmouth, and Harvard were all examining the highs and lows facing businesswomen like Judith who were contemplating comebacks.

Judith fit the profile of a Wharton study that had interviewed women who had taken breaks from managerial or professional careers but were looking to return to some kind of corporate position. The woman they described now preferred to work in a smaller, more entrepreneurial environment. She had continued to network by keeping up relationships with friends and former colleagues from her business world. And she had either maintained or developed skills in her time away from work that would be useful on her return. Judith's school fund-raising fell neatly into this category.

More than 80 percent of the women in the Wharton study took lower positions than those they had left. Judith fit this profile, too. In fact, she differed from many women in that she reversed a trend. Many businesswomen in the study who went back to business tried to start their own business. Judith had had her own business before she quit. Now she decided she didn't want the responsibility. Her choice was to be an employee.

She had the full support of her family in her decision. In fact, they were her biggest cheerleaders. No one felt the family might be short-changed if Judith were to work. Her children wanted her to be out and about in the world. They were so proud of her, they wanted to show her off. They wanted her to shine professionally—they wanted to share her.

Returning to full-time work was much harder than Judith had imagined. Just physically sitting at a desk for five days a week took its toll. She got backaches, she gained weight—she wasn't able to get to the gym as often, so she quickly felt out of shape.

One of the first things to go out the window on rejoining the workforce is physical exercise. Do stay-at-home mothers do nothing but go to the gym? Of course not (contrary to what my own daughter might have thought). But they can usually find the occasional hour or two or three during the week to work out, particularly when their children start preschool. Mothers who go straight back to work after a maternity leave and who want to exercise have it built into their routines from the start, usually getting it over and done with early in the morning or at lunchtime.

But mothers who return to work after a long time at home can find they know how to do their jobs and how to take care of their kids, but they're not quite sure how to take care of themselves. Where are they meant to find that time? Should they exercise before work? Then how would they get their kids to school? Even if their husbands could step in, are the mothers sure they want them to? They want to see their children in the mornings. Isn't the idea to lead their own lives *around* their kids not instead of them? Lunchtime? Not enough time. Maybe enough to get your nails done, or a haircut or color if you push it, but forget exercise—too time consuming when you factor in the shower. Evenings? Too tired.

It's another handicap caused by a lack of confidence. Unlike their colleagues who never leave the workforce, women who return to work aren't confident enough to take extra time out of their working day for themselves. They are not at the level where they feel they are entitled to take a longer lunch or get in a little later in the morning. They have to work extra hard proving themselves all over again.

They know if they exercised more, they would feel fitter, have more energy, probably weigh less, and look better. They exercised regularly before and can see and feel the difference. They miss the lift their moods got from working out. Often women see exercise more in terms of looks than health. They might feel ashamed that it matters to them. They think that taking care of their bodies is an indulgence, not an imperative. Some of them actually put exercise on their calendars, scheduling time at spas and ashrams or taking hiking or tennis vacations throughout the year. Here they push and exert themselves like camels, storing up healthy food, massages, and physical activity in the hope that the benefits will last more than a few days. "I neglect my appearance," said Judith despondently over breakfast one morning on her way into the office. She was eating an egg-white omelet as part of another ongoing diet. "You look good, you need time. You have a lot more maintenance at this age!"

Judith scheduled a visit to Canyon Ranch and even went by herself for a week at a California ashram, which turned out to be a little more hard-core and less pampering than she was prepared for. Being Judith, she often made friends and business contacts on these trips. Sometimes the contacts she made turned out to have lucky consequences—like the time she found the financing source for Warren's brush business during a stay at Canyon Ranch.

Despite having little time for herself, Judith finally synthesized a feasible balance between work and home. She would get up last in the household—a luxury in itself. She wasn't a morning person and no longer had to be one. The kids got themselves up, and Warren would get everyone breakfast. As they left she'd get up in peace. Maybe she'd make it to the gym, maybe she wouldn't. She'd be at the office between nine and ten, work through the day, often with a lunch break. Then if she didn't have some kind of evening professional event, she'd be home at about the same time as her children came back from school.

There was much about her job that she liked: she met a lot of exciting entrepreneurs, she liked the intellectual challenge, the feeling of having her own life, and the chance to be doing something different; she learned a lot about new technologies and how those deals are structured. She liked that she didn't have the sole responsibility for the company as she did when she ran her own business, but instead could leave at the end of a day, or a week, close the door on work, and not think—or worry—about it. But there was also much that she didn't like. She felt that she could have done more stimulating or challenging work. She felt that she had rushed into accepting a salary package that didn't reward her when she performed beyond her own initial expectations. She also felt too far along in her career to be working for someone else—and too used to doing things her own way.

She was at another crossroads in her life, but this time it was different. There was no urgency. She felt less strongly about things. She was able to relax more. She had a life outside the office that she enjoyed. She felt as Nancy Astor once said," I used to dread getting older because I thought I would not be able to do all the things I wanted to do, but now that I am older I find that I don't want to do them."

Yet her kids, with their own urgency of youth, had higher standards for her. They were so used to her being the queen bee in their lives, they couldn't understand why she didn't play the same role at work. Both of the twins felt guilty about it. When at the end of two separate interviews with them I asked them if there was anything they still wanted to say, they each made the same points, though in their own distinctive styles.

Katie announced that she thought her mom was a lot smarter than her colleagues realized and she "probably deserves a higher position in work." She also felt that Judith "clipped her wings just a little bit" because of staying home with the twins. "She's *really* smart," said Katie earnestly. "I know she's trying to make a compromise and she could work part-time. I know she doesn't want that full-time crazy working experience, but I know if you want the higher position, you're going to have to work like that, and she doesn't want to give up the time with us."

Robbie made similar points. With great passion he told me, "I love my mom and I see so much potential in her. And I feel like I shipwrecked her. She was a powerful working woman. I was born with my sister. She stopped working. I felt terrible about that. And then she had to come back working with people who were younger than she is. And doing much less than what she was used to." When Robbie described Judith, he sounded like the preview of the next Hollywood blockbuster. "She. Is. An. Amazing. Woman," he declared. "She has so much potential. She is this energetic person; she's so smart, so brilliant."

But all the family felt that, in Robbie's words, "she is lower than she should be." They understood that is the way it had to be, coming back to work. "You can't start at the top again," Robbie pointed out. But their brilliant Judith should be doing better. They wanted her to earn more—in terms of both money and recognition. They wanted her to take risks.

I found the twins' aspirations for their mother enormously touching. I loved the idea that children could be ambitious for a parent rather than the other way around. When I told Judith what Katie and Robbie had said, she cried. So did I, and we both sniffed and sighed together as we reflected that one element of a successful comeback should include proud kids.

A few months later I met Judith for coffee outside her office. It was the beginning of summer, the sun was shining, and we sat in a Midtown plaza with a fountain close by and felt quite civilized. The Feder kids were all about to take off for their various summer destinations, sports camps, trips to Europe, beach time.

What had crystallized for Judith in the intervening months was her desire to stay in what you might call the "real" world of work. She felt she could take on more responsibility and more autonomy while earning more money, and more respect. As she talked, she described the atmosphere in her office, and for the first time I really appreciated what a male-dominated environment she worked in. Everything was a battle. She felt she didn't get enough respect and had to fight to get percentages of deals that were owed to her. A coworker begged her in front of several other workers to call Brooks Brothers and return one of his suits. Another needed her help with buying an engagement ring. She was asked to buy clothes for kids' trips, choose flowers for Valentine's Day, and pick out gifts for a mother. Yet if one of her kids called in distress, one man, who was the parent of three kids, might indicate his impatience at the intrusion, if the call came at a bad time. "They don't have to think about home when they're at work," was Judith's comment on the double standard.

Much like her kids, I began to feel outraged on Judith's behalf and continued to do so until I realized that Judith didn't feel the same way. I was reminded of Eleanor Roosevelt's line "No one can make you feel inferior without your consent." The atmosphere in her office didn't make Judith feel put upon or put down. On the contrary, it made her feel more confident about her own abilities. She felt she could easily hold her own in this world. She had achieved her primary objective. She had come back.

Maxine Snider

What do we live for, if it is not to make life less difficult for each other?

George Eliot

HERE'S A DILEMMA that a growing number of women are facing: what happens if a mother goes back to work and her career really takes off? Let's say she has decided she wants to be her own boss and finds she's really good at running a business. The flexibility and autonomy of being in charge fit well with the demands of a family. As her children grow and leave home, the business remains. Often it grows, too. Instead of feeling the pang of the empty nest, she welcomes the extra time she has to work without guilt. She might find she's unexpectedly in one of the happiest, busiest, most demanding, and most rewarding times of her life.

What happens if that happy, busy time coincides with a new emptiness in her husband's life? I'm not speaking of the departure of his children but the period of his retirement. What then happens to a marriage? In discussions about work and family we tend to think that "family" means children. But what about husbands? How do you balance your husband's needs?

Maxine Snider has had to answer this question. At the age of sixty-four she is the sole proprietor and designer of a boutique business and designer of a highly stylized furniture design collection. Her office is based in Chicago, and her pieces are sold in showrooms around the country. Like many small businesses, hers began with small steps. In 1977 she was working as an interior designer. A decade later she was designing most of the furniture for a client's new house, and in 1999 she decided to make furniture design a full-time career. By 2005 she had designed three collections and was running a two-million-dollar company with two full-time and two part-time office workers, contracting the work out to furniture builders, upholsterers, and artisans in the Chicago area and beyond. In those seven years her furniture range grew to include writing desks, screens, beds, chaises, end tables, and benches. In the summer of 2006 she added nine more pieces to her collection, expanding its scope and line. There was now an armoire, two sofas, an armchair, new tables, and a "French" desk. You could buy Maxine's furniture from Chicago to New York to Los Angeles. It was all beautifully designed, sleek, and expensive. And its designer personally approved every detail on every piece before it was shipped to a client.

If Maxine refers to her furniture as classic, her story is trend-setting. Yet it has been set against the more traditional professional life of her husband, Larry. And as you'll see, her success was due in large part to his. Like many women, she was able to make choices because of the salary her husband earned. His financial stability meant that she could take risks.

In 2004, just when his wife's business was moving into top gear, Larry Snider retired from a thirty-two-year career practicing bankruptcy law. He was ready to enjoy his own second stage—a stage that was thousands of miles, both literally and figuratively, from the relentless grind of his legal career. For most of his adult life he had worked at the pace of a driven man. As the founder of his own large law office in Detroit, then as a senior partner in the enormous legal firm of Mayer, Brown and Platt in Chicago, he billed top dollars for long hours to some of the country's best-known corporate names. And now? Now he wanted to take long, leisurely trips to exotic places where the pace of life could be considerably slower. He wanted to indulge his passion for photography, to take hours over a meal, to sit, to look—to just *be*.

Men with careers like Larry's are a dying breed. Rather than retiring, we're all going to keep going and going. Federal census projections tell us that in 2015 "older workers" of fifty-five plus will make up 20 percent of the labor force. In about five years' time there will be well over 30 million of them. We live longer and need more money. We can no longer afford to quit work two-thirds of the way through our lives. Retiring at sixty-five is becoming—old. This means that men like Larry are becoming anomalies, just as women with careers like his wife are becoming more and more common.

Maxine is doubly trendy—she's an "older woman" who owns her own business. Another look at the federal figures tells us these are the ones to watch. Women like Maxine might not be running the world, but they are taking over the workforce.

Small businesses owned by women are growing at double the national average. You may have to redefine your notion of small. Mine *was* one, two—maybe ten or so employees, definitely well under fifty. Down at the Small Business Administration they aim higher. They call a business "small" if it clocks in with up to five hundred workers on its books. Small businesses owned by women are anything but small. The latest government figures showed well over a hundred thousand women-owned firms with annual receipts of $1 million or more and close to ten thousand businesses generating $275 billion in gross receipts. And these numbers are almost ten years old.

The idea of being your own boss after time out of the workforce is understandably appealing for several reasons. First there's the situation you've become used to at home. While you might feel you're at everyone's beck and call each time you set foot in your house (and each time you leave it, seeing as they all have your cell phone number), you do actually run the show. You decide who does what, when. You manage the time and often balance the books. You tell everyone what to do. It might be tactless to say that you *own* this particular business, but you certainly manage it.

Once you're comfortable being a boss, it's hard to imagine returning to an environment where you have to report to one. It's not so much being told what to do; it's more about when you get to do it. You know you can write the report, plan the pitch, or design the software and get everything back on time. But if your son has a soccer game, you want to go—without asking for permission—and catch up later. You can always work at night. One thing having children gives us is an awareness of the twenty-four-hour day.

According to the women's office at the Small Business Administration, most businesses owned by women do start out as being genuinely small. It's just you, or you and your sister, or maybe a neighbor working in your bedroom, kitchen, or basement after the kids have gone to bed. It's much more convenient to turn on your home computer than to drive back into a more conventional office after dinner. "We always tell 'em you have control over your life. *But.* You have to understand you are not going from a forty- or sixty-hour week to anything less. You'll just—sometimes—be able to have more control over the hours. Which means you'll never sleep," said Wilma Goldstein, of the office of Women's Business Ownership of the Small Business Administration.

Another advantage of running your own business is that you don't have to get a job as such. You're already hired! By yourself! Now the only way you have to sell yourself is as part of the package you're offering. Women who lack confidence often find it easier to be an advocate for a product, a service, or another person, rather than for themselves. And if you truly believe in your business idea, you don't have to look for confidence. You've already got it.

Maxine Snider has confidence. It's hard to imagine her without it.

It's as much a part of her style as her silvery hair—not colored nor short, but kept smooth and long. Her eyes, enormous and turquoise, make their own strong visual point. Her elegant clothes and subtle jewelry project the confidence of good taste. In a 1999 interview that she gave to an interior design magazine about her own apartment, she said, "I've always thought great design comes from knowing what to leave out." Now, that's a confident remark.

Yes, she knows what to leave out. But she also knows what to put into an interior, right down to the smallest detail. Her home is a large duplex apartment that is welcoming and warm. Think of the style as haute bohemian. Dark-stained wood floors, china from Ireland, bits from China, a chair from Peru, and, of course, immaculately folded towels, perfectly stacked by height order in the bathrooms.

When artfulness is intuitive, which is what having a good eye is, you're off to a good start. But an artistic instinct doesn't necessarily translate into an instinct for business. Like most people, Maxine learned her business sense on the job.

She was born in 1942 in Philadelphia, the second child and only daughter of Samuel Bobman—a small business owner himself, whose trade was men's clothing. Her mother, Lillian, who was thirty when Maxine was born, was a homemaker with a love of art. From the time Maxine was very young, her mother took her to Saturday art classes as a way of passing on her own passion. Lillian was a traditional housewife, whose home was the medium she used to express her own artistic inclinations. She was a keen decorator, who experimented with decoupage and made some of Maxine's clothes. But her ambitions didn't extend outside the house except for the education she arranged for her daughter.

The Saturday art classes were just the tip of the iceberg. Throughout her childhood, to college and beyond, Maxine felt her mother's support as she opened door after door in her professional life. Lillian had no career ambitions for herself, yet she believed her daughter should lead an emancipated life. It wasn't such a surprising double standard. Maxine was born when America was at war and the roles of women were in flux.[1]

If studying art has an air of privilege to it, it is true that the family had begun to prosper. Samuel Bobman hadn't gone to college. As a young man of twenty, he and his brother had started selling army and navy gear. After a while he went out on his own, eventually opening a popular menswear chain. Maxine and her brother, Herb, enjoyed the advantages of their father's newfound wealth. They moved from the city to a larger house in a Philadelphia suburb. Herb went to private high school and then on to Wharton. Maxine went to Lower Merion High School, a prestigious public high school in Ardmore, Pennsylvania.

Maxine wasn't just artistic; she was also a bright student. By 1960 there was no question as to whether she would go to college. The question was where. Her parents wanted her to go to the University of Pennsylvania as a commuter and live at home. But, unsurprisingly, the idea didn't appeal to her. "That wasn't like going to college," she said. "I knew they wouldn't support the idea of living in the dorm. My parents were very old-fashioned in a way." She wanted to study art, but she also wanted a college education. At that time Cornell and the University of Michigan stood out as places were she could get both. Maxine claims that while she inherited her love of art from her mother, her love of a bargain and her attention to the bottom line came from growing up a child of her father's retail business. In weighing her college choices, it struck her that Michigan, being a state school, was a tremendous deal, even for out-of-state students. "That became my argument, so they said, 'You can go and stay for a year.' "

Unlike many parents of this time (or any time), Maxine's believed she could make art her career. "Other parents, of some of my friends, could only see art as a hobby. You also needed an academic concentration or a teaching degree," she said. "My parents also felt that I was not going to college for the purpose of finding a husband. It was to end up a finished product so I could earn a living and they believed I could do that with art. This was very unusual for the times."

Early during her stay at Michigan, she took a couple of design classes. She liked the structure of "seeing everything through a frame," of planning an image. She became interested specifically in graphic design during a junior year internship she won at Detroit's Campbell-Ewald advertising agency. Today Campbell-Ewald is a juggernaut of an agency, the sixth largest in the country. In the fifties it was smaller but undoubtedly a cool place to be. Like most agencies in Detroit, its client life revolved around the car industry— Chevrolet was its biggest customer. Every year the agency took a group of undergraduates and on the first day of the internship gave them an invented assignment that had nothing to do with cars— and that year it was to develop a campaign for Hershey's chocolate. The Hershey Company had never advertised with anyone, so the entire project was fictitious. Maxine loved it. "The people were so hip," she remembered. "The whole setting was like that. It was so much more exciting than what was happening in college."

As anyone who has watched the A&E series *Mad Men* knows, graphic design (the explanation of an idea using a visual medium) was expanding both in form and application in the late 1950s and 1960s both in Europe and in the United States. From paper to posters to signs, from illustrations to advertisements, from typeset to corporate logos, from pen-and-ink to printing, from two- to three-dimensional images, graphic design both represented and participated in the 1960s cultural explosion. Graphic design went hand in hand with advertising: if you took a degree in graphic design at college, you would almost certainly be looking for a job with ad agencies at graduation.

In the September of her second year of college, Maxine was waiting for a table at a restaurant with a friend. A handsome man approached them and said they could sit with his friend and him. Larry Snider was in his second year of law school, four years older than Maxine. At the time, he acted like "a real jerk" (his words), who thought Maxine was attractive but didn't follow up on it right away. Still, the two of them started dating sporadically. At Christmas she went home, and he missed her so much that he realized he was in love.

From January to March Maxine and Larry were completely inseparable, and in March they were essentially engaged. Maxine had an emergency appendectomy, the month before Easter break and her mother came out to Ann Arbor to be with her. Larry had already arranged to visit Philadelphia during Easter break to ask her father's permission to marry her, a visit Maxine was well enough to make with him. They were both astounded when her father said yes and to this day neither of them can explain why he gave his permission so quickly, given Maxine's young age of nineteen. They were married in Philadelphia in 1962 in what they described as a traditional white wedding "with all the trimmings." When they moved into an apartment together in Ann Arbor, Michigan, Maxine didn't decorate it— she didn't need to. Larry had done the whole thing for her as a surprise.

Larry Snider had his own strong aesthetic sense. The son of a Detroit businessman who worked in both real estate and the meat business, Larry was the kind of undergraduate who was ambitious but unmotivated while in college. When he graduated he decided to take the money he had saved from his bar mitzvah and go around the world. He had minored in Far Eastern studies and was fascinated by Japan. In Ann Arbor he met Kimi Tojo, whose father had been prime minister of Japan in World War II. Kimi suggested that he live with a family to really see Japanese life and Kimi's wife arranged for him to stay for a time with an affluent family. The father loved to paint and took Larry to private Japanese art collections. "I had an incredible experience that changed my life. But instead of continuing the trip for a full year, I decided to go to law school. I was running out of money."

After law school, Larry was finally ready to settle down to a career. But he never lost the appreciation he had gained for the visual arts. Throughout their marriage this common ground has been a powerful connection for the couple. That Larry decorated their first apartment and that Maxine actually enjoyed and appreciated what he had done tells a large part of their story. This shared sensibility gives an otherwise fairly competitive couple a place to meet and be creative. It's not that their tastes are exactly the same, but they are discriminating enough to create a world with room in it to indulge both their preferences. This passion for all things aesthetic has anchored them in their long marriage.

By the time Maxine graduated from the University of Michigan, Larry had found a job in Detroit at a small general practice law firm with a specialty in bankruptcy law. His salary was fifty dollars a week, and he could keep any money he brought in from business. Bankruptcy law remained Larry's area of expertise for the rest of his career. After five years he had done well enough to gain the confidence, desire, and ambition to be his own boss. In 1968 he formed a law firm with a friend, which grew to seventy lawyers by the time he left in 1991.

Meanwhile, when Maxine graduated from college she was "really impatient to work." She took her portfolio to a number of ad agencies. More than once she was told that the agencies liked what they saw and to hang on for "three weeks or a month" until a slot opened up. Three weeks or a month might seem like a nice opportunity to take a vacation or just kick back and take it easy, but to a graduate in a hurry it seemed like an eternity. Maxine approached a family friend, an architect, for advice. He looked through her portfolio and noticed a presentation board covered in fabrics from a course she had taken in interior architecture. Students had been asked to show everything from a floor plan to a completed rendering of the project. Maxine ended up using her work to decorate the couple's second apartment when they moved from Ann Arbor to Detroit. The architect told her she should take that board around to architecture firms and offer her services as a designer. She did and immediately got an offer from a firm to join their interior design team for one hundred dollars a week. She accepted.

A great story—except she hated it. Every day when Larry picked her up from work, she had a pounding headache. He told her she either needed glasses or she hated her job. "I got my eyes checked. I did need glasses but I still hated my job." Part of the reason she didn't enjoy it was that her work was limited to the design of schools and hospitals. "I was gaining a lot of basic experience, but it didn't have the excitement I associated with design." She wanted a broader exposure to a range of projects. She figured out that the best way to do this quickly was to offer her services as a freelance design consultant to smaller groups of architects. A smaller firm, she reasoned, probably wouldn't have its own in-house designer. She could come in on a project-by-project basis.

With the confidence she now attributes to youth, she quit her job and managed to line up three different small firms to work for. To offset the unpredictability of freelance work, she got a regular part-time job in the design department of the enormous J. L. Hudson Company department store, on Detroit's Woodward Avenue. The forty-nine-acre store boasted an art gallery and a fine wine department. On the top floor was a contract design studio, serving clients with commercial projects. The range of work made it interesting; it was possible to do everything from a laundromat to a high-level executive office.

What was it like for a woman to work in commercial interior design in the 1960s? It was a world of opportunity for Maxine. America was building. With urban landscapes exploding, skyscrapers were sprouting up everywhere. Male architects still took care of putting the buildings up; female designers came in and made them look nice.

So Maxine's parents had been right. They'd believed her artistic

talent could lead to a professional career, and it did. From the time
she graduated from college, she was able to earn a living from her
creativity. The artistic world she entered was not the world of the
garret but the world of the office, with contracts and deadlines.
From the start, her approach to her career was businesslike. Yet she
always combined a desire to succeed with a need to feel fulfilled in
what she did.

In 1966 Maxine went to work for Walter (Wally) B. Ford II. Ford
was a forty-four-year-old member of the motorcar family with a degree in architecture from Yale University and a background in product, exhibit, and interior design from General Motors Styling. In
1948 he had founded W. B. Ford Associates, a firm that specialized in
"space-planning, interior design, corporate identity and graphics,"
as the Ford & Earl Web site now puts it. Two years before Maxine
joined him, Wally had merged his company with the design firm of
Harley Earl, a famous General Motors designer, who had once sum-
marized the marriage between creativity and commercial by saying,
"I am sure we all realize how much appearance has to do with sales."
Over the next few years the new company created interiors for newly
constructed buildings, like Rockefeller Center, the World Trade Center, and Detroit's MichiCon building. They did the offices for RCA
and the newsroom at the *Washington Post*. They even did the drawings for the film set of *All the President's Men*.

A junior designer in the company at twenty-five, Maxine had a really glamorous job. She worked on the lobby of the World Trade
Center. She designed the interior of the First National Bank of
Chicago (now JPMorgan Chase). She was involved in everything
from the executive offices, to the general office floors, to the dining
rooms. She even conceived the wall murals for the bank's cafeteria.
She worked on the executive offices for the Ford Motor Company's
world headquarters and the Manufacturers and Traders Trust Bank
in Buffalo, New York.

Her success was helped in part because she was being personally mentored by Wally Ford himself. He found it amusing that she was chronically late, and had taken her under his wing. "He thought I brought another dimension to the team," she said. "In those days I was responsible for choosing interior finishes, fabrics, and furniture, and the men were responsible for the architecture and the mechanical aspects." She also benefited from a relationship that the firm had formed with the Japanese architect Minoru Yamasaki, the creator of the World Trade Center. Yamasaki used Ford & Earl for many of his interiors. His appreciation for her style was to become useful later in her life.

Maxine had no children to make demands on her time while she worked. The Sniders waited seven years to start a family. Maxine felt she was young enough not to rush; she was busy enjoying her work and building her reputation. Her hours were long, she often stayed at the office till late at night, and she traveled a lot. Larry was also working hard building his practice. In those days the couple had an active social life together but didn't see much of each other alone. "Every Wednesday I would fly to Chicago," Maxine said. "We were like ships passing in the night. We were so busy, we don't have any recollections of that time. We were pursuing different goals. My memory of it is that we weren't in conflict—the marriage was the air we breathed, but we certainly weren't working at it."

One winter she caught a bad cold that lingered and lingered and eventually turned into mono. Maxine felt ill, weak, and dispirited. She decided she had been working too hard, and when she returned to work after a month of being at home sick, she asked Wally to let her work four days instead of five, which he agreed to. She began to think more about her personal life, about how she was giving all her energy to work. She began to think about having a child. Being forced to slow down helped her transition to the next stage of her life.

Stephanie was born in August 1969. Maxine was twenty-seven. She had thought she would like to be at her firm for about five years before getting pregnant, so that if she did take time off, she would be asked back. She then stayed home for seven years as a full-time mother and did not return to work until Suzanne, her second daughter, was three years old.

By now, Larry was earning a considerable salary. He was the father who got up early and drove into the office, spent the day there, came home for dinner, and disappeared into his study to work some more. He was not, by his own admission, an involved parent. "I think Larry was consumed with the anxiety—with the demands of his work," said Maxine.

Maxine loved being a mother. She wanted to enjoy her house, do her flowers, play with her baby, and be present in one place. She didn't want to "flit back and forth." With the birth of Stephanie, she felt her identity change and she relished her new domestic self. She was comfortable and unconflicted as a full-time mother. "When Stephanie was born I was absolutely enraptured. I had been working for seven years. People would say to me 'Do you miss your work?' And I would say, 'Not at all.'"

Did she think she would never work again? She didn't think about work at all. Both her head and her heart were at home, and she didn't want or need to contemplate any future stages.

Three years after Stephanie, Suzanne was born in 1972. Shortly afterward the Sniders moved from downtown Detroit to a suburb twenty-three miles from Larry's office. Larry described his day like this: "I tried to make it a habit to get home for dinner at six thirty p.m. We had a guesthouse on our property, which became my office. I would work from eight or nine p.m. till eleven. I read papers, I would dictate. I'm an early riser, so I would get to the office by seven. I get up at five or five thirty. Many times I would get up earlier and go to the office at three or four a.m."

Suzanne said that though he came home for dinner every night, he would rush the family through their meal so he could do the dishes and get back to work. Often he would fall asleep sitting at the table. His children didn't notice him as being much of a presence, but their mother was always around. "As I child I never felt like I had stolen or rushed moments with her," said Stephanie. "I always felt I had enough time with her. She was very attentive."

The three-year gap between her children meant that by the time the younger daughter started preschool, Maxine had been at home for seven years. Larry described a moment (possibly apocryphal) when on the morning of Suzanne's first day at school Maxine went into the house and called Minoru Yamasaki for a job. Just like that.

There was a reason it was all so easy. In the years she had been at home, Maxine had kept in touch with Wally Ford, going into the office for sporadic visits and occasional lunches. Ford had said there would always be a job for her at the firm should she choose to come back. She was a known and valued commodity. Her design skills were in place. She could come right back in and pick up on a new project. Yet when she did decide to work again, she chose not to return to Ford & Earl but to go over and sign on with Yamasaki. Why? "Wally's office was forty minutes from my house. Yama's was ten. Wally's would have been a much better working environment, but it was a much longer drive, and I didn't want to do that."

It was a mistake. But it was a natural one. Like many working mothers, Maxine wanted to be home more, and she thought the shorter commute would give her that extra time. What she didn't realize was that the friendlier working environment actually would have been a better bet. She negotiated a thirty-hour workweek, which was designed to mean she could leave the office at 4:00 p.m. and be home shortly after the girls got back from school. On paper it was perfect, but from the start it was a disaster. Working "on loan" to Yamasaki from the Ford company had been a completely different experience from working directly for him as an employee. "It was killer trying to work thirty-hour weeks. He [Yamasaki] was demanding and mercurial. The memory of the confict is so palpable. It was painful." She found her new environment to be completely sexist. "Even the women were sexist. If you are a woman, you do X," which was essentially clerical work. As for the men, "they were such guys." During this time, she discovered that she was not good at dealing with the guilt of being away from her children. And she also realized that "I was not the mom who could go to work for another person and have another person set the rules."

Meanwhile, she wasn't particularly thrilled with her child-care situation. The girls were at school—Suzanne for the morning, Stephanie the full day. Maxine tried out a few helpers—students from the nearby community college—before settling on a full-time housekeeper who lived in for part of the week and could cover for her till she got home. Lula was a warm, loving young woman, who Maxine described as Suzanne's "stand-in mom." "It felt okay that she was with Suzanne," Maxine remembered, "until I started to come home regularly in the winter to two children propped in front of television, *in the dark*!"

This wasn't what Maxine had imagined in her parenting plan, and the combination of dissatisfaction with her job and her child-care arrangements led her to think about becoming her own boss. In fact, the decision made itself. When Maxine decided to leave Yamasaki after "one and a half years that felt like a hundred," she hardly had to think it through. As she says, she just did it. You could call her lucky—she was fortunate enough to have the financial cushion of Larry's income to sustain her. But the income obviously came at a price. There's no such thing as free money. Larry was so busy earning a living that he was scarcely at home. Who knows how much she felt she needed to be there for her children because of his absence?

By the time Maxine decided to go out on her own, she had formed enough connections to get work easily. Her field remained commercial interiors—she had yet to decorate anyone's house—but the scale of the buildings she worked on became smaller, and they were closer to home. She became more of a suburban than an urban decorator. It amused her that her final project for Yamasaki had been the airport pavilion for the Saudi royal family in Jedda, Saudi Arabia, when she found herself working on a local dentist's office in Bloomfield Hills. Even so, it felt right.

She created her own office on the family property. It was the late 1970s, and she put her own stamp on her space: track lighting, charcoal gray carpet, big white drafting tables, and file cabinets, with architect's lamps dotted around.

Because her clients came by word of mouth, they were all a short driving distance away. She designed offices in industrial parks, worked for banks and realtors, and created the new building for the Jewish vocational service. In many ways she was doing exactly what she had always done, but it had all shrunk. The work was smaller, nearer, and she was the boss. Travel had been reduced to visiting sites that were all within a few miles from home. She might still be working when her children came home, but she would be around, and they loved going in to see her. They both have warm positive memories of her home office. "I loved her office," said Suzanne. "She was very generous about her space. I would go there and Xerox my notes. I typed up all my college applications there."

From 1977 to the late eighties Maxine ran her own design company. In doing so she was conforming to the career pattern of many of the women in her business. In her book *Women of Design,*[2] Beverly Russell points out that of the thirty-three interior designers she profiled, only three worked for large firms; the rest ran their own companies.

Maxine didn't advertise, do public relations, or bother with marketing her services. She didn't have to. The work flowed in—and so did the money. She didn't need Larry's money as a cushion after all. At her peak she was making about one hundred thousand dollars a year which she kept in her business. She didn't need to contribute to the housekeeping or the mortgage. Larry took care of that. He still paid all the bills—in both senses. He wrote the checks and earned the money to cover them. For a brief period Maxine took over the actual paying of the bills from a household account, but Larry got anxious when she didn't pay them immediately (she waited to do all of them once a month), so he resumed the task. A career dealing with bankruptcy can have an impact on your sense of financial security.

Maxine had enough work to hire two part-time employees. She was so busy that at one point she decided she needed to cut back. She had reached a point where so much work was coming in that she would either have to expand her business or reduce the number of jobs she took on. "It wasn't about being ambitious," she said as she explained her decision. "Your work has to fit with your idea of yourself. Equilibrium is my highest priority and I know my limitations."

Ironically, achieving that equilibrium might be harder for a mother who is self-employed than for one who answers to a boss. The buck invariably stopped with Maxine. I liked the way she looked at her choices, though. She knew she could do whatever she wanted. She could have a booming practice if she wanted one. But she knew that that choice would come with its own price. If she wanted a balance between her work and her family, she would have to take a little of the time and energy that her work demanded and put it into her family. This was her choice. Because she was her own boss, she could make that choice and implement it. Just because you can do it all doesn't mean you have to. It means you can choose from it all and do what works for you.

Maxine cut back once, but the business grew back. Over the years, there were times when she felt she was so busy that she was just treading water, just keeping her head above the surface of all the demands on her time. So much was required of her. But being at home, with the girls' school and her job sites close by, meant that for the ten years while her children went from elementary to high school she could be around when they needed her.

Still, after ten years of hard work Maxine needed a break and a chance to recharge her creative batteries. As her teenage girls began to look to their own futures, Maxine thought about hers. The creative process doesn't always benefit from a life led at full speed. Sometimes it helps to do nothing—"nothing" being a relative term. Maxine decided to slow down completely and reinvent herself as an artist. She gradually wound down her business to devote herself to painting for a period that began as an indefinite ending but turned into a five-year sabbatical, working in a much more private and personal way. In a statement she wrote to accompany an exhibition of her work in 1990, Maxine said that when she painted, "Everyday objects take on a new meaning, a new opportunity." This statement was to take on its own meaning when the next chapter of her life opened up.

Larry had been unhappy in his legal partnership for several years. Having grown so large, his firm was at its own crossroads. The direction of its expansion was an area of contentious debate among the partners. In 1991, with the girls en route to college, he and Maxine decided to make a huge change. He sold out his interest in the law firm and accepted an offer to run the bankruptcy department at Mayer, Brown and Platt, at the time Chicago's largest law firm. He was fifty-two years old.

It was a life-changing move for the couple, but their lives were already different. They were just a couple again. The girls had left home—Stephanie for the Rhode Island School of Design, Suzanne for Wesleyan. It was unlikely that either of them would be coming back to Detroit. Larry and Maxine talked over their future for six months. What did it mean to be empty nesters while so young? What should they choose to do? They were planning how to live the second half of their lives.

When they decided to go for it and leave Detroit for Chicago, they chose to make a move into the future and middle age together. This was not necessarily how they had lived their lives previously. Their marriage had existed largely on two parallel paths. As such, it had at times felt lonely.

Larry's love of traveling coupled with a fear that he was being entirely consumed by his career had inspired him to take up photography in the late 1970s. That and a canoe trip to the Peruvian jungle in a moment of midlife crisis led him to take regular trips to places ranging from China to Ecuador to Ireland. Sometimes Maxine went with him, often she didn't.

Moving to downtown Chicago from suburban Detroit as empty nesters represented a return to the kind of life they had led as young newlyweds. Only now they had more money, and since Maxine had wound down her business, she had more time. They bought a large duplex apartment in the Gold Coast neighborhood, a block away from Lake Michigan, and began an extensive renovation. Larry now had a place to show off his enormous photography collection, which he had been building for years. He had thousands of photographs, including works by Henri Cartier-Bresson, Diane Arbus, and August Sander. Many of the photographs are hung in even lines and double layers throughout the apartment, giving their home the feel of a domestic gallery.

Maxine ran the renovation of the apartment. She had found space in a building near the apartment where she had her painting studio, but doing the plans for her new apartment made her realize that she missed design. She was also adjusting to the reality of life in Chicago. Suddenly she was in a new city as a middle-aged woman with no identity other than that of being her husband's wife. In Detroit she'd had an established name as a designer, two children, and a lifetime's accumulation of friends. She felt their absence with the move. "When I moved here with Larry, he positioned himself in a law firm as a senior attorney, and had an instant identity and I had instant invisibility," she said.

"I was very worried about my mom when I was in my first year of college," said Suzanne. "Because the house [in Detroit] for my mother was a metaphor for her life." But, she added, "She's so resourceful. She perseveres and thinks of a way to do anything."

When some friends who were building their own house in Michigan asked Maxine to be their decorator, she balked at first. But after her Chicago apartment was finished she decided to accept their offer. The project—her first as a residential designer—took three years and marked the beginning of another career. During the course of the renovation, after hunting unsuccessfully for some particular pieces of furniture she wanted, she sat down, designed them herself and then had them made. It felt easy and exciting. When the house was finished, she stood for a moment in the kitchen with her client and said out loud, without realizing what the words meant, "You know what? I think I am going to design furniture."

"It was completely a moment," she remembered. "The immediate reaction of the client went a long way to making the idea real. He said, 'I think that's a great idea.' "

Why did she find the idea of furniture design so appealing? "When you are working with a client doing an interiors project, to do a good job you have to be personally involved in your client's lives to some extent; which always made me a little uncomfortable. Painting, on the other hand, is very solitary. This was a perfect way of designing the things I love and working in the way I feel most at home."

She went to Larry and told him of her idea and asked him if he'd like to invest in her business. His immediate reaction—influenced by a life of dealing with businesses in trouble—was to ask her if she had a business plan. It was a reaction that she found hurtful and dismissive, and she never asked him for money again. "I said yes I do have a business plan. My plan is to be a success. But that was his opportunity to invest, and he lost it."

In fact, Larry's reaction hadn't been as dismissive as Maxine thought. It hadn't been dismissive at all. He explained, "This was the most natural thing in the world for me to say. It meant I took it seriously. I dealt with companies looking to restructure, and I always said, 'Put it down on paper and we'll take a look at it.' I don't think that Maxine knew that about what I did for a living." Whatever the misunderstanding between them, Larry was actually very supportive of Maxine's talent and her plan. It was in his interest to be: he wanted her to be happy.

Arriving in Chicago might have made Maxine feel invisible, but it also gave her the energy to do something about it. She was fifty-five years old and felt ready to remake her identity. The hiatus, the change of surroundings, her age all led her to experience a renewed creative rush. "There are huge rich resources here [in Chicago]. There is a strong design community, great architecture—and the energy that goes with that. I thought I could find a place that would make me visible again and happy."

With ideas of furniture buzzing around her head, and Larry on a photography trip along the Silk Road in China, she decided to go to Paris and came back with what would become the *Paris Series* of furniture. She had done ten drawings she described as "wood and upholstered furniture designed in a minimalist spirit with a nod to the past." Furniture design is a strange business. You start with an idea. You draw that idea. As Maxine said, "My thought was that with the initial collection I would honor details but reintroduce the collection as modern." But then what? Unless you are a carpenter yourself you have to find someone who can take your drawing and build a desk, a table, a chair. Then you have to sell it. But who will be your clients? How will people get to see your products?

And how do you pay for all of this? Maxine was the sole proprietor of Snider, Inc., her decorating business. When the company was doing well, the money flowed in and she kept it in the business. So when she changed direction and moved toward furniture design, she became (without her husband) her business's sole investor. Her previous business subsidized the prototypes for her new one.

There are a dizzying number of stages in the furniture design business, each involving their own decisions. What should a table be made of? How will a chair stand up and not fall down? How many drawers should there be in a desk? What about the finish? Where should the handles come from? Who makes them? Are they priced right? Sometimes, when your focus is keen and your energy high, you can accomplish the impossible. As Maxine set out to answer each of her questions, she slowly learned the basics of the design business. Each answer led her to the next question and the next stage.

She found a woodworker by reading the paper. "I was reading the Sunday *Chicago Tribune*, the House and Home section, and there was an article called five woodworkers to watch. I picked one from his profile, Charles Spreitzer. I told him I had a short deadline. He was a sculptor not making a living, so he was making furniture. I went to his shop and showed him my drawings. He got it."

"It's kind of cool she wasn't a young artist when she came to me," said Spreitzer, who described Maxine as "not a dreamer; she'd been around the block. Usually you don't want to run into an interior designer that's just starting to make furniture. They come to you with ideas for stuff that can't be made. I wasn't too worried about Maxine. She had a lot of questions, but her drawings were great."

From her work as an interior designer she knew of the importance of having her furniture seen if it was ever to be bought. Her business instinct ran in strong tandem with her creativity, as it had done throughout her career. In December 1998 Maxine joined the Chicago Furniture Designers Association (CFDA), a small group of locally based designers who met once a month in a restaurant to "gripe" about their work. It was through the group that she learned of the first opportunity to have her work seen.

A local gallery owner, Judy Saslow, closed her gallery every spring for a couple of weeks and lent it to the CFDA to show their work. Each person was permitted to show a maximum of two pieces. This was Maxine's moment and she knew it. She sat down and quickly drew a sketch for the Paris writing table—a desk that has turned into one of her best-selling pieces. "I drew it in about an hour. It just came together so comfortably. Then I drew the Paris side table." She got a good enough response from the two pieces she showed at the

Judy A. Saslow Gallery to feel she was capable of taking the business to the next stage.

The Chicago Design Show—a furniture expo for people in the trade—was coming up, and she decided to be in it. She would create ten pieces of furniture, some of which would be upholstered. Upholstering furniture is a different subset of the business from making desks, wardrobes, chests, and tables. She found an upholsterer by word of mouth. Everything was coming together.

It was then that she had a moment that might be familiar to many women: "A woman who was at the show looking for a showroom in San Francisco said, 'I want to represent your pieces.' I said: 'I'm not ready.' She said: 'Why not?' And I thought, *Why not?* Then I thought, *You wanted to do this, so do it!*" So she sent her samples from the show to San Francisco. From that representation she got hooked up with a showroom in New York.

Not every piece flowed as easily as the first. She had lapses in her confidence and kept thinking she would be "found out." She was worried that people would discover she wasn't really talented. Still, she was able to keep up a momentum that sustained her through her failures of nerve. When she got her first order, which was for the dressing stand and mirror, she did think "how easy this is."

Once she was represented in showrooms in San Francisco and New York, she felt strongly that she should also be represented in her hometown of Chicago. She met the showroom owner and furniture designer Holly Hunt at an early convention, and asked her to look at her work. Hunt said it was good but not a large enough line for her to represent. A couple of years later, when Maxine had added more pieces and had more of a track record, Hunt took her on in Los Angeles, Miami, and Chicago.

If you're a furniture designer like Maxine became, you don't sell your pieces to the general public. Instead you sell to the "trade." Her clients were now interior designers. She knew what the market wanted, because she had worked in it. The stages involved in getting furniture to an interior designer are as much a part of the business of being a furniture designer as getting the furniture made in the first place. It's a little like the plot of the children's book *If You Give a Mouse a Cookie*, by Laura Joffe Numeroff. This is how it works: If designers are going to buy from you, they have to know about you. So you have prototypes of your pieces made and then photographed. Then you put together marketing information, a press packet, and maybe design a Web site (www.maxinesniderinc.com). Now your photographs are ready to be seen, but you need people to see them. So you hire a PR person to get your name into shelter (decorating) magazines, and then you mail out the clips from those magazines to other magazines so that they write about you, too. You take part in furniture conventions. You might take on a consultant. If you do all that and your pieces end up being bought, chances are you'll have spent so much money you won't be able to pay yourself a salary.

Like many small business owners, Maxine never thought of paying herself a "salary." Even when she was doing well at interior design she hadn't given herself an annual income. This was why Larry thought of himself as the family's breadwinner. Until 2007 she had never given herself a regular paycheck. Though her business is profitable, she prefers to plow the profits back in, hiring people to take some of the office work off her shoulders and reinvesting in developing new pieces.

One sunny spring day, I flew down to Chicago to spend a couple of days shadowing Maxine as she went about her business. She took me to lunch at the Arts Club, where she is a member, and we chatted together as we drove out to Brusic Rose, Inc., the local company that handles her upholstered furniture. Brusic is a family-owned third-generation furniture business, the bulk of whose clients are designers and architects. The company does a lot of custom work, but it is also set up to process six or seven hundred pieces at a time. Maxine tends to order selected pieces in quantity, because it is cheaper. The company can then store her pieces (unfinished) until needed. Brusic is as invested in finding a winner as Maxine, and they work with her to finalize the design. The company generates a full-size drawing from her draft, which they transform into a computer version and then onto a finished couch or chair prototype. It's a collaborative process, and Maxine loves it.

We were there to inspect some of the new prototypes they were working on together. The company had just moved into a new building, and the atmosphere was fairly chaotic. One of the finishes on her chairs was the wrong color and didn't match the sample she had left with them earlier. There was a couch that wasn't ready for her to inspect, though this was the reason she had come out.

In all, the trip was more a waste than good use of her time. She was impressively nice about it. Impressive because while it was clear that she wasn't thrilled by the inefficiency, she was able to make the point without being ruffled or unpleasant. She stated that the color was wrong and then got someone to find the right sample and give it to the finisher. She arranged for the finisher to refinish the chair. She wondered—nicely—when the un-upholstered sofa would be ready while conveying her enthusiasm for the work that had been done. She was patient and understanding about the disorder caused by the move. She accepted the excuses—excuses that were almost, but not quite, apologies. She told the manager that she sometimes worried that they had so much of her business, but that her worries were offset by what a good job they did.

Afterward in the car she said, "Everything's working well there at Brusic, but they are falling behind schedule." This was a valid concern. Brusic made *all* of her upholstered pieces. If she fell behind on orders because Brusic was putting other (bigger) clients before her, she would be forced to look elsewhere for an upholsterer. She would stay with them because she had a great relationship with the company's manager. The two of them spent a considerable amount of time together, even on the day when I was there. I watched as they took their time examining the difference of a half-inch on the base of a sofa and then picked out mohair and cording to cover it.

Maxine completely came alive as she talked on the floor. She hadn't been made angry about the delays, because she enjoyed being at the plant. She was energetic and vivacious. She knew her own mind but was also genuinely interested in what the builders had to say. If they could improve a piece, then they should.

Maxine's success has been both her blessing and her curse. By 2006 she had reached a point in her furniture business that was similar to one she had earlier as an interior designer. Once again she had too much work to handle. Should she expand this time? It would be harder to reduce her volume of business. When orders came in she had to fill them. It was hard to know what to do. Broadly speaking, she had three options: close down, expand, or try to keep going at the same level. Which road should she take?

"We haven't been doing this long enough to have all the answers for that," said the SBA's Wilma Goldstein when I asked her about Maxine's predicament. "A lot of us are concerned with this. We have these what we call 'lifestyle businesses,' because they match the lifestyle of the women who do 'em . . . There is a big group that may not want to have a multimillion-dollar business, they just reach that point where they either shut it down or expand it." A couple of years ago, Goldstein said, companies that had grown to this point were given a name: mezzanine businesses, because they had reached the next stage.

Maxine's dilemma was complicated by the fact that Larry had just retired. He was now free to take off on the lengthy trips he had been dreaming about, and he wanted his wife with him. The way he saw it, this was not the time to be thinking about expanding a business or even working at all. Maxine was in her early sixties and had as much choice as she'd had at any other time in her life. But as before, her decisions would carry their own costs. *What should she do?*

She took all of her questions to Rae Terry, a smart, friendly furniture consultant with decades of experience in her field. "The first thing I said to her, which I have said to every client I have ever had, is, 'What do you want this to be?' " said Rae Terry.

She answered that she loves how the company is going, obviously she recognized the fact that it is difficult for her to be the CEO, designer, sales manager, and marketing person and to do all of those things. But she has never felt that she has the financial wherewithal to hire someone to come in and do the sales and marketing end of the company. I think she does place a high value on her life with her husband and her personal life, and therefore she feels a little conflicted about that. But I know she would like to see the company grow in terms of sales volume.

Terry felt that Maxine was at the point where she should start looking for outside financing. With an infusion of cash, she could hire people to run the sales end of her business, have an ongoing advertising program in the high-end shelter magazines, and even own some of her own manufacturing by investing in the companies of the people who produced her pieces. "All of that is about having a serious business," commented Rae.

But then there was Larry—pulling her in the opposite direction. "If she weren't in her business, we would be living differently. I want to go to ten different places and live somewhere for a month. One winter we tried to take a week's vacation every month (as a compromise). It was terrible. We did it last year; we tried it, and I said I am not going to do it again. I could travel by myself, but in some of these countries you get lonely—you want to share it with someone."

He didn't exactly come out and say it, but he made it clear that she had a deadline to finish working full-time on her business. "I told her, 'You need an exit strategy.' She said, 'I am thinking about it.' When the business was smaller, I told her the exit strategy was liquidation. Now that her sales are up to that number, the exit strategy would be a sale."

Maxine was able to resist the arm-twisting of Larry's not-quite ultimatums, but it was harder to turn down the appeal of the travel. A month in Peru or India? Wasn't this what life was supposed to be all about?

Somehow we expect that all of our choices make our lives easier, but they can also make them more complicated. A previous generation of wives would have taken off around the world with their newly retired husbands without question. Were these happier marriages? Were these happier women? Maxine wasn't unhappy, nor was Larry. But they were both used to living life on their own terms. What they needed to find was a balance, a way of compromising. They were still looking for equilibrium even as their children had long left their home.

At first, the solution to their quandary seemed to present itself in the perfectly timed reappearance by one of their daughters. Both women were busily pursuing their respective careers, Suzanne as a writer and teacher and Stephanie as an artist. Having graduated from Yale and the Rhode Island School of Design, Stephanie taught sculpture part-time in Baltimore, and later at Princeton. Now in her thirties, she supplemented her income with work as an interior designer. She was still single. One summer, she agreed to fill in at Maxine Snider, Inc., when an important staff member took maternity leave. She came to Chicago and spent three months living at home, working in the business. Maxine hoped that she would come to love it and consider joining the company.

But the appeal for Stephanie was not so much a career in Maxine's business as a chance to help her mother and spend time with here. The two have always been extremely close. Working with Maxine gave Stephanie the opportunity to see her mother in her own light as her own person, but she didn't see working in her mother's business as a permanent option. As much as she enjoyed the summer, her first priority remained her career as an artist.

Wouldn't it have been nice to end one of these stories with a mother handing her business down to her daughter? In this case, life didn't work out that way. Stephanie ended up being offered a full-time faculty position at the Rhode Island School of Design and continuing her work as an artist. She exited this chapter to pursue her own future.

The next time I checked in with Maxine, several months later, she sounded much happier, calmer, and less conflicted. "I totally love doing this," she said firmly. "And it doesn't feel like work. I have a much more stable situation with our shops now and that makes all the difference. They know what they have to do, and I don't have to manage it all, which was stressful."

"I love to travel," she added, "But I'm not worried about negotiating that with Larry anymore." What had changed? As it turns out, Larry had. Or to be more accurate, Larry's circumstances had. As Maxine put it, "He didn't even *need to work at* backing off." Larry's photography was receiving wider recognition. He had three galleries representing him and his work was included in numerous museum collections. In 2007, Doug Dawson, of the prestigious Douglas Dawson gallery, contacted Larry to ask if he would supply some of his photographs to decorate his booth of Asian artifacts at the Asian Art Fair at the New York Armory. Dawson took nine prints, sold six, came back and told Larry he wanted to represent him.

Larry's photography now had a greater sense of purpose. He felt motivated to work harder and Maxine did not resent his trips to various places around the world, all of which made him less demanding as a husband. He still wanted Maxine to come on trips with him, but he realized that he was better off alone if he wanted to be productive. So they worked out a solution where she would accompany him to a foreign country for a couple of weeks, and then he would stay on by himself and work.

With Larry's photography taking some of the pressure off her, Maxine felt far less torn. The couple still planned to travel. Their next trip together would be to Japan. Before they left, Larry would spend several months of happy hours reading Japanese history books and travel guides as he looked for historical sites and artifacts to photograph. Once there, they would combine their time together and apart. He would take pictures, and she would look for inspiration for new pieces of work. "I think we both realize that if she wasn't working, she would be much more demanding of my time," said Larry, cheerfully, with no sense of irony.

In the meantime, business was booming at Snider, Inc., and in a gratifying twist, Suzanne, the younger daughter, made time to write for the company Web site, giving it an infusion of cool with a new blog. Maxine joined showrooms in Aspen and Atlanta. Hotels were now taking notice. Calls were coming in from the Greenbrier Resort in Virginia, the Four Seasons Hotels, and the Breakers Hotel in Palm Beach. This new attention meant her line was being produced on a much larger scale. Her sales rose by another million dollars.

She didn't need to look for outside financing.. The business was easily covering its own expenses. She made it clear to her suppliers that they would need to expand their businesses as she expanded hers. "I don't want to hold back to fit the shops," she said as she prepared to celebrate both her sixty-fifth birthday and her forty-fifth wedding anniversary. "My goal is to grow."

Sherry Goff

There are no second acts in American lives.

F. Scott Fitzgerald

We will just have to die when we're thirty.

Zelda Fitzgerald

SHERRY GOFF HAD been a teacher all of her working life, so when she decided to go back to school and train as an occupational therapist after her time at home with her three daughters, she didn't think she'd face too many problems. After all, she'd never really left education. But her first shock came in her first class. Retaking chemistry after twenty years, the forty-three-year-old Sherry, who now wore reading glasses, found it wasn't so much that she couldn't understand the text, but that she couldn't even *see* it—the print was too small.

It's a cute little anecdote, this one about the aging mom bumbling through the chemistry class. It's the kind of story you might expect when you think about baby boomers retraining for the second half of their lives. You can just picture her squinting at the symbols, wondering what the hell she's going to do.

So what did she do? This incident took place almost fifteen years ago. Sherry's had a life since then. When I talked to her, she was keen to point out that it hasn't been a particularly unusual life, "I'm not Superwoman," she said.

No, she's not. Instead she's a woman with an encouraging story. She's a mother who's had two different careers, each one requiring its own specialist training. Her two careers occurred on either side of raising her kids.

Sherry might not be Superwoman, but it would be nice to think of her as everywoman. She's funny and smart, and clearly terrific with children—her own and everyone else's. She's pretty and young-looking in her mid fifties, with light brown hair and laughing eyes that glint at you through her glasses. You can imagine her at a parent-teacher conference, telling you things about your child that you might not have noticed yourself. She's the teacher who can explain both long division and poetry, whose kids sit still and do their homework, whose classroom is organized and colorful.

Her teaching career ended when she was in her thirties, but Sherry still works in schools. Today she is an occupational therapist employed by the local education authority in Midland, Michigan, where she lives with her husband, Barclay, a traveling salesman, and their dog, Gracie, a black Labrador. Her widowed mother, Carol, has a house a few streets away. Sherry's three daughters, Norah, Molly, and Hannah, are grown and gone to their own lives. Norah's an attorney in Kansas; Molly's a teacher in Portland, Oregon; and Hannah's an engineering undergraduate at the University of Michigan at Ann Arbor. They stay in touch by e-mail and phone, and their photos are all over the refrigerator in the kitchen, where they appear as a good-looking, closely knit trio. The sisters combine a mix of the strong dark coloring of their dad and the more delicate, petite lightness of their mom. From the numerous typical family group shots, it looks like everyone in this family enjoys a joke.

If you think that taking time off work is an option only for wealthy women, then take heart. The Goffs have had their share of hard times. There have been periods in both Barclay's and Sherry's lives when they were unemployed and unable to find work. This is a family that has had to balance its books and figure out its priorities. The picture the Goffs present has a kind of Norman Rockwell quality, with hard work and scholarships, soccer games and church groups, with mission trips, strong family bonds, and deep friendships. The Goffs have never had a lot of money, but they have put three kids through college. Their lives are supported by a sense of community that revolves around their Christian faith, specifically the First United Methodist Church.

Sherry was born in Peoria, Illinois, in June 1951 to Ray Bornsheuer, a twenty-three-year-old mechanical engineer on the Santa Fe Railroad, and his twenty-one-year-old wife, Carol. Carol had worked after high school and in the early days of her marriage as a secretary in a legal office. Once Sherry was born, she stayed at home with her daughter, and a couple of years later she and Ray had a son, Bill. Back then there had been no thought of Carol going to college, although she had been a good student. "But there was actually just no chance for me to go, but it didn't bother me because no one else was going either." As she put it, "The goal of every girl in my high school was to get married."

After a couple of job relocations for Ray, the family ended up in Topeka, Kansas, where they stayed for the rest of Sherry's childhood. There is a stability to the early part of this story that reflects the time in which it was set. "Back in the fifties the big thing was to keep a clean house. And that was life. And it wasn't all that bad, either," remembered Carol. Ray engineered bridge and track repairs for the railroad for forty-one years—from the time he was seventeen years old until his retirement in 1984. "The days of a man going to work and working for forty-one years at the same place like my husband did are over," said Carol, who was married to Ray for forty-eight years. "Ray went to work, he got a good pension, and I was taken care of after he died. That wouldn't happen now."

If that stability has disappeared, it has been replaced by choice. It's quite something to see what different lives the three generations of women in this family have led. Even Carol's own life changed dramatically after her husband died. Whereas once she had been completely dependent on Ray, never needing even to fill up the car with gas by herself, she developed the confidence to drive herself longer distances, made friends online in chat rooms, and flew around America on trips to the West Coast and Florida—even to Europe. "I don't think she did the finances at all, never did the taxes. She didn't know how to navigate insurance," said Sherry, talking about her parents' marriage. "He did all the grocery shopping after he retired. She never drove at night. He took care of the house, the typical male stuff. The repairs. She did all the cooking. He did the grilling."

That was their relationship, one in which they were both willing participants, and they were completely happy together. Still, "their world was small," said Sherry, and they didn't travel. Since becoming widowed, Carol has literally climbed mountains—in Germany. "I remember when I was young, she wouldn't even look out of the window of the car when we drove up a mountain in Colorado," said Sherry. "Her world has broadened so much."

Carol was always a passionate quilter, and today her house is filled with enough quilts and batiks and pieces of embroidery to look like a small shop. All of that gives it an old-fashioned charm of a time gone by. Yet there are strong touches of modernity. She is technologically right up to speed. She makes quilting patterns and family albums on her computer. She even likes to watch *Sex and the City*, and occasionally she sounds like one of its characters. "You go from one phase of life to another and everything changes, and if you can't change it and accept it, you are really screwed," she told me as she offered some more of her home-baked orange loaf.

Like others in this book, Sherry was the first in her family to go to college. She was a bright student, bright enough to get a National Merit Scholarship. Back then college didn't cost so much. Still, Carol

went back to work as a secretary to help pay the bills when her children were in junior high school. If the family had had more experience
of education after high school, they might have been a little more ambitious in their choice of college for Sherry. It was enough for them to
set their sights on the University of Kansas, which is where she went.

After graduation she went into teaching, but it was not her first
choice of career. In fact, the nice irony of her story is that her
first choice ended up becoming her second career. Before her junior
year, Sherry knew she wanted to be an occupational therapist (OT).
She liked working with people, she was interested in medicine, and
she felt occupational therapy was a broad enough field to give her a
number of choices. In those days, OTs worked mainly in hospitals
and nursing homes. They were less of a presence in schools. So she
was looking at a profession where she would be dealing with adults
rather than children.

She changed direction after she interned with a professor who
worked in special education. It was 1973, and the concepts of behav-
ior modification and mainstreaming children with special needs
were just coming to the forefront. Sherry's professor got her a job
team-teaching with another of his students in an elementary school,
and as a result she ended up majoring in elementary education. Her
first career was set.

Barclay Goff wasn't thinking too seriously about his own future
when he met Sherry. He was a hard-partying frat boy, the son of a
college professor, a big jock who had a job—not a career—laying
carpets in a trailer factory. Barclay was the kind of man who let decisions make themselves. Like the decision to get married, for example. "We lived together for a while and then Sherry asked why we
weren't married, and I couldn't think of any good reasons, so we got
married. And it was the right thing to do." Professionally, the young
Barclay had the same easy-come, easy-go attitude. He got a job at
the local lumberyard. "I was just working along at the lumberyard
and then I went into management, and we didn't want to move, and

then we decided maybe it's time if I want to get ahead. If you wanted to get ahead, you had to move. So we moved."

It was the moving that changed the professional balance within this marriage. At the time of their wedding Sherry was making more money than Barclay, and she did so for some time. When Barclay got a management position at the local lumberyard, his earnings began to match hers. And then when they moved, she had to quit her teaching job and find another. For the next several years he made more money than she did.

The issue of who makes more money is crucial when parents decide who spends time with the children. It goes right to the heart of equality in a marriage. Barclay's period as the larger breadwinner coincided with the arrival of the Goffs' children, so it was a natural choice for Sherry to stay at home with her girls. Yet he did not always outearn his wife. He didn't in the early days of the marriage, nor did he later. During those periods Sherry had to work. In Barclay and Sherry's marriage, the fact that the financial scales tilted up and down between the two spouses created an equality that can sometimes be missing in other marriages in which one spouse continuously outearns the other. If a husband or wife earns a large salary with benefits, an expense account, and a company car, it can be hard for the other partner to feel that his or her smaller paycheck is valid—or valued. If your salary is much less than your husband's and barely covers the cost of child care, do you end up staying home even though you'd rather be working? If so, do you feel that you really had a choice—or a voice?

Barclay was—and is—the kind of husband who enjoys his wife and her life and their time together, without questioning who is meant to do what in a marriage. The roles are set. They both work, but she has primary care and concern for the children. He wishes she didn't have to work so many hours or days at her job, because it can be a struggle for her to find time to take care of the house. He's never been the kind of man who thinks he might take on some of his wife's domestic duties.

He might have become that kind of man if he had stayed as liberal as he was in his youth. But he didn't. Today he is far more conservative, a change he attributes to having listened to hours and hours of talk radio while on the road. For several years Barclay has driven around Michigan as a salesman, along the way becoming an enthusiastic fan of Dr. Laura Schlesinger. He even gave a copy of her book *The Proper Care and Feeding of Husbands* to his wife one Christmas, much to her disgust. When I asked him how he knew Sherry was right for him, he invoked Dr. Schlesinger. "She said, 'A woman chooses a man she can live with, and a man ends up with a woman he can't live without,' and that's how we got together."

They got married in 1975. After Barclay moved into management and started making more money, the couple eventually reached a point where they could consider living solely on his salary. Norah was born in 1977, then Molly in 1981. By then Sherry was thirty and had been teaching for almost ten years. She decided she wanted to stay home with the girls, and though money would be tight, the family could manage.

Religion was always present in their lives, but only in a "medium strong" form when they were younger, said Barclay. He had grown up in a Congregational church, and Sherry was a Lutheran. As newlyweds they didn't attend church. It was only when Barclay took a job managing a local lumberyard in a small town in central Illinois that their religion became more important to their lives. The town had a population of about five hundred, 75 percent of whom were Catholic. "And right away I was the lay leader," said Barclay, "and Sherry was running the Bible school."

Joining the church was a way of getting to know people. Until the move, Sherry had lived in Lawrence, Kansas, a forty-five-minute drive from her mother. Carol had been able to step in and help with the kids when she was needed. When she moved to Illinois, she lost the family support system. She had moved into a small tight-knit community, but it wasn't what she was used to. "The teachers were the only college-educated people," she recalled. Most parents in this small community were in their very early twenties—more than a decade younger than the Goffs. There was "not much of a peer group."

When the girls began school, Sherry decided to go back to teaching and managed to do so without a problem. She got back in first as a substitute teacher, then when a spot opened up, took the sixth-grade class. Her fellow teachers became her friends. The school and the church were the social centers of her world. At this point, work was more of an antidote to isolation than a financial necessity.

In 1987, when Norah was ten and Molly was eight, Barclay was promoted again in a move that took the family to Midland, Michigan, where they still live. Midland is the home of the Dow Chemical Company, which had been founded there ninety years earlier, in 1897. It's a pretty, small industrial town. Driving toward it, you cover flat land where the sky stretches out above you, seemingly close enough to touch, creating a sense of infinite space. Within the town, the evidence of money generated by Dow is everywhere, from the state-of-the-art Grace A. Dow Memorial Library, to parks, schools, and well-kept streets and houses.

On their arrival, Sherry immediately started looking for a job and for a church to join. The church was easier to find. The First United Methodist Church was one of several large, busy, active churches in town. It was an enormous center of worship, one of the largest Methodist churches in the state and the social linchpin to hundreds of families in the area. Many had come to Midland as transplants, brought there by jobs at Dow. Those who had left their parents and siblings behind in other states, or other parts of the state, relied on the church as a surrogate support system. Congregants met one another at Bible study groups or potluck dinners. Kids became friends at Sunday school and on mission trips. The Goffs joined a young couples group that they now joke should be called Old Couples. Ninety percent of the friends they made and still have come from that group, according to Barclay.

Meanwhile, Sherry's job hunt wasn't yielding much. She found herself looking for a teaching job in a market with few openings and plenty of other experienced, well-educated applicants. She was briefly able to work as a substitute, and then as a part-time teaching assistant in a preschool. This was not what she had envisaged as a career, and it was a disheartening state of affairs.

The solution was unexpected and unplanned, and it took her right off the career track. In 1988, while still searching for a full-time teaching position, Sherry discovered she was pregnant again. In early 1989 Hannah was born—a late surprise to her thirty-eight-year-old mother, who decided that with two school-age girls and a baby daughter, she both wanted and needed to be at home.

This time around Sherry was not a typical stay-at-home mother. Instead she got a license and turned her home into a small day-care center with a few local kids coming every day. Providing day care gave the family an additional income when their expenses were rising—three girls are more expensive than two, and middle-school girls are more expensive than toddlers. It also allowed Sherry to be at home with her baby and released her from the frustrations of job hunting. Yet this work was clearly a job, not a career. Eventually it led to her decision to go back to school to retrain.

You can take the teacher out of the classroom, but you can't take the classroom out of the teacher. Sherry's day-care routine was fully planned with activities, trips to the park, and games both outside and in. Hannah loved it. From the time she was born until she went off to kindergarten, her house was full of friends and toys. She never needed to go on a playdate, as they all took place in her living room and yard.

Running day care, and no longer looking for a teaching job, made Sherry realize that she no longer wanted to teach. But after a few years she didn't want to be a day-care provider, either. She was home all day, but she never stopped working. Unlike teaching, day care meant she had to work summers, which she didn't like. Being there for other people's kids meant she had no time at all for herself. Children would be dropped off and picked up by their parents on their way to and from work, which meant Sherry's workday began at about 7:30 in the morning and didn't end till about 5:30 in the afternoon. Grocery shopping—any kind of errand—had to be taken care of in the evenings or on weekends. She had no flexibility and not much of a professional future, either.

During this period Sherry's parents moved up to Midland to be near their granddaughters. "When we got here Hannah was four, Molly was eleven, and Norah was in high school," said Carol. "We babysat any time we could. We were mighty happy to have the girls and would have them over anytime we could." Sherry now had the family support system with which she had begun motherhood.

Meanwhile, Norah was about to head to college, and Molly was becoming increasingly independent as a junior high school student. They would need Sherry less and less. So when it became Hannah's turn to go off to kindergarten, Sherry decided to go back to school, too.

She had never forgotten her desire to become an occupational therapist. One of the mothers who used Sherry's day care happened to be an occupational therapist herself. She told Sherry about a new training program offered in OT at Saginaw Valley State University about thirty minutes away. SVSU had been founded in the early sixties to answer a growing local need for educated scientists, engineers, and teachers. As a result, it offered a number of educational courses emphasizing professional training. The timing of Sherry's interest was one of those lucky breaks. In the early nineties, when Sherry was brooding over her interest in OT, the university was expanding both its courses and its enrollment. There was a course available that lasted for only two years and led to full accreditation in the career she wanted. She thought and she prayed, but the decision seemed obvious. "I was on a church retreat for women, and I just decided at that point that that was what I was going to do."

Today SVSU offers a five-year program leading to a master's degree as opposed to a two-year program leading to a bachelor's degree. Five years is a long time to spend in school when you're in your forties. Would Sherry have applied for that length of course? "Five years would have been too much—and too expensive!"

Once she had made the decision to retrain, Sherry had to figure out *how* to do it. This was something she "prayed like heck about." "Sherry does the research," said her best friend, Deb Morgenstern. "She found out what was necessary to do it, what she could do, where she could go, how they could finance it. She took charge and she accomplished."

She went from providing day care to needing it herself. The Goff family now had a daughter in kindergarten, a daughter in middle school, a daughter in high school, and a mother in college. Though she got some hours credited because of her previous degree and experience, Sherry was looking at two and a half years of not earning an income, just when her oldest daughter was about to go off to college herself. Even though Barclay's parents were able to help out a little with money, it was a really tight period—particularly after the first year, when both Norah and Sherry were in college.

With the possible exception of Hannah, who hated the fact that she now had to go to day care after school, the whole family stood united behind Sherry's college plans. Sherry was old and experienced enough to understand that Hannah would be fine. She had her older sister, Molly; she had her grandmother; and she had her dad. She was at school. Her mother wasn't working long hours, and she wasn't far away. She'd adjust. "I remember talking about how we were going to swing this," said Barclay, as he described how they saw the fork in the road. "I think I said, 'You should do this.' I knew we weren't at the top of the hill right now, and we needed to do something to improve ourselves, and this was it." "This was kind of an investment," added Sherry.

She was a few years short of the zeitgeist when she went back. During the summer of 2006, the American Association of Retired

Persons (AARP), in conjunction with the American Association of Community Colleges, did a mailing of thirty thousand respondents age forty-two and older and found that 26 percent who had begun a new career in 2005–2006 had taken courses toward a college degree or certification.

Partly connected to this finding, a number of stories began to appear in newspapers and magazines about the "new trend of retraining." "As Older Students Return to Classrooms an Industry Develops" ran one headline in the *New York Times*,[1] while the *Wall Street Journal* wrote, "Across a range of industries, many companies desperate for qualified employees in a competitive labor market are creating . . . retraining programs, hoping to recruit experienced workers from other fields. And workers, from lawyers to longshoremen, are finding the intensive courses make it far easier than it used to be to begin a new career."[2] *Newsweek*'s "Back to College for Retraining" made the point that "Community colleges offer older workers an affordable way to reinvent themselves and find their place in a changing economy."[3]

Books started to appear on the subject of "Career 2.0" with titles like *Portfolio Life: The New Path to Work, Purpose, and Passion After 50*,[4] and *Second Acts: Creating the Life You Really Want, Building the Career You Truly Desire.*[5] Boomers were bombarded with hip marketing buzzwords to describe lives such as "new adulthoods," "second acts," "third ages," "near elderlies," and "encore periods." Middle-aged workers were urged to start picturing their careers in terms of wheels rather than ladders or pyramids.

Markets were opening up for the newly retrained in nursing, technology, education—even air traffic control. The New England branch of the FAA began offering a "second career program [for] older adults who have completed their child rearing and related family responsibilities by the time they enter the program. The services provided by the second career program include vocational counseling and assessment, training, monitoring client progress, and placement services."

Retraining in midlife has been said to have two main benefits. The first is that for people—like mothers—who haven't worked for a while, it is easier to look for a new job with a new diploma or degree. Second, with boomers living longer and social security running out, a worker who retrains or gets a second education will work longer and be better able to take financial care of herself than one who hasn't.

The National Science Foundation sponsored a study by two social scientists and found that midlife education both protects middle-aged and older workers from job loss and offers them more "job mobility" as they age. In other words, education can continue to expand horizons as you get older, just as it did when you were young. But the study had a more ominous point to make. Workers who don't retrain are at risk of losing their jobs. While in the old days a "good initial education and occupational achievement were market advantages that protected middle-aged workers from job insecurity . . . this may no longer be the case." As Sherry's mother pointed out about her own husband, the days of working for forty-one years for the same company until you retire are over.

The Goffs knew they were buying a certain amount of financial security with the course that Sherry was on. The chances that she would get a job that paid more than the three hundred dollars or four hundred dollars a week she had been taking in as a day-care provider were good. They also knew she needed to do something with her days more challenging than taking care of kids in her living room. Sure it was a risk, but the pros definitely outweighed the cons. They had no idea how beneficial their decision would prove to be. In the short term, Sherry had to take some classes before she could be eligible for the OT course. This provided the family with a kind of dry run for what life would be like with their mother back in school. And it gave Sherry a gradual reentry back into the classroom.

Did going back gradually make it any easier? A little. But being the same age as the forty-three-year-old teacher in a class full of eighteen-year-old students is a tough adjustment, even before you open the chemistry book with the tiny, incomprehensible print. OT had developed a lot in the decades since Sherry had first considered it. The biggest change was in the use of technology as a supplementary aid. Unlike the teenage students who came to SVSU from high school, Sherry had no technological experience at all. She was computer illiterate, and had never needed an e-mail account. Now new software programs were constantly being introduced to make life easier for those with disabilities, particularly children. Kids who couldn't hold a pencil might be able to tap a keyboard. If they couldn't hit the keys, they might be able to speak into a computer and "write" that way. Autistic kids who worked with therapists had a wide range of programs to help them, too. Not all of them were on the computer, there were DVDs and flashcards as well as CD-ROMs. But you needed a computer to buy them, as they were only available online.

Instead of separating children with special needs into their own schools, school districts now encouraged the inclusion of all kids into a mainstream classroom, with occupational, physical, and speech therapists coming in and helping out during the day. Parents were encouraged to supplement the help their kids got at school with additional programs at home. They could go onto the Internet and download games or print out pages for their children. They could order their own sets of CD-ROMs. A good therapist needed to keep up to date with what was on offer and know how to work collaboratively with what was being done at home.

Developments in medicine had produced a generation of kids in the late 1990s with different challenges from those in the 1970s. For example, there had been a rise in the incidence of autism. And babies with birth defects who might once have died—like the Feder twins—were surviving and growing into school-age children. OTs work inside and outside of schools, helping kids with sensory processing problems, learning disabilities, cerebral palsy, autism, and other developmental disabilities to become more independent. Their ultimate success is when a child no longer needs their help.

Sherry wasn't sure she would be working with children or in schools once she got her degree, even though with her teaching background it was an obvious direction for her to take. Local education authorities hired a finite number of OTs to work in their schools. Someone had to leave before a vacancy opened up. This had been the problem when Sherry was looking for a teaching position. No one left; therefore, there were no jobs. But, unlike teachers, OTs aren't confined to working with children. Sherry could look for a job in a hospital or in private care, at a nursing home, or in assisted care for the elderly. In the meantime she concentrated on getting her degree.

Despite the fact that she had to retake chemistry, had trouble reading the small print, and couldn't even type, she loved her studies. She liked the students, who were a tight-knit friendly bunch, and she loved learning about how the brain works. She would be able to work with one person at a time, focusing on an individual rather than a group. And perhaps best of all, she'd have some flexibility back in her life.

Hannah hated it. She hated the day care at SVSU. She hated the fact that her home was no longer the center of the universe. And she hated the fact that her mother had her own life and she didn't see her as much. "I was really clingy, and I was used to having my own group of friends at my house every day, so I think it was a tough transition." The older girls, with their independent lives, were impacted less. But at the end of the course everyone had one last big adjustment to live through. Sherry would be spending an entire summer out of state on a required internship.

This was the worst part for Hannah. "I know that that summer was really hard for me. My room was really, really messy all the time. My sisters were both home, so they were the female influence. They didn't get along, so that was hard. We ate a lot of fast food. My dad wasn't the cook. But my grandparents lived in town, so they were involved a lot." In fact, having her parents nearby was a real advantage to Sherry. It meant she could consider internships located farther away, and there were relatively few to be found. She cast her net as far as Kansas City, where her brother and his wife lived and she could stay for free. She found a hospital internship for the summer and prepared to move.

The Goffs are a family who travel by road, not air. Flying is prohibitively expensive. Cars packed full with kids, clothes, and books cover long distances on trips that are regarded as adventures in themselves. Barclay and Sherry packed up the car and took Sherry and all her stuff to Kansas in May 1996, stopping for a nice weekend break in Chicago en route. Barclay's mother had recently died, and Sherry was able to use her car.

The summer experience was surprisingly evocative of her undergraduate years back in Kansas. She still knew a number of people in the area and she re-embraced her single life. She worked every day, and on weekends she still had time to eat out a lot, read, and spend time with her old friends.

Part of the reason she was able to immerse herself so completely in this temporary new life was that she could afford only two trips home in three months. She recognized that though this was an enjoyable sabbatical from domestic life, it was "a hardship on the family." Hannah remembered, "I would talk to her on the phone. She came home halfway through and then left again, but that was kind of weird to have your mom come home to visit you. She didn't come more, because she would have had to fly, and I know that money was tight at that time." Three months might seem like an eternity to a six-year-old, but it is still only three months. Once the internship was up, Sherry would have to move back home, take her board exams, get certified, and find a job.

Sometimes there comes a moment when some kind of divine intervention swoops into a life and helps out. Maybe it's luck, or maybe we make our own luck. However you want to interpret it, this was

the moment when Sherry got a lucky break. The same mother who
had told her about the course at SVSU now called with an urgent
message. There was an opening for an occupational therapist right
in the Midland school district. One of the therapists was taking a
year's leave, and the job would be available at the beginning of the
school year in August. Sherry should fly up to Midland immediately
for an interview.

It sounded too good to be true. If Sherry got this job, she would
be working in all the schools in her neighborhood. She flew straight
home, despite the unplanned expense.

Applicants for the job were coming in from all over the place, including one man from Detroit who impressed the interviewers with
his extensive pediatric experience. The interviewers found Sherry
impressive, too. They liked her friendly confidence. They saw the
value of her years in the classroom. They appreciated that as a
mother she would work well with parents. Still, she was not their
first choice. They offered the job to the pediatric candidate from
Detroit.

Sherry didn't know this at the time. Nor did she know that he declined the offer because it didn't pay enough. All she knew was that
a call came through telling her she had the job. She couldn't believe
how lucky she was. "I still think what would I have done if I hadn't
got that job, because jobs were really hard to come by. I don't know
what I would have done."

Hard on the heels of the lucky break came a tougher one. As she
began her job she had to deal with the declining health of her father.
"Right after she got home from her internship my husband got
sick," said Carol. "It was pneumonia and he was getting better. All
of a sudden he got worse, and I took him to the emergency room,
and in three weeks he was just gone. This happened right when
school started, and Sherry spent a lot of that time with me at the
hospital. That was a hard time for her. She loved her dad and she
needed to do it. She wouldn't have been able to stay away."

If the timing of losing her father in the first weeks of her new career was awful, at least Hannah was happy. Sherry had been assigned to a handful of local schools, one of which was Hannah's elementary. Now mother and daughter were back on the same premises, finishing their working days at about the same time. From Hannah's point of view it was a perfect reunion.

Sherry had to study for and pass her board exams, which she did. The exams were in March, but she studied on and off for the whole year. Instead of becoming a complete reinvention—as some second careers can be—Sherry's new life was a synthesis of everything that had come before it, even down to her earliest career ambition. It was a satisfying situation, pulling together everything she had ever done while taking her forward. The risk of going back to school had paid off.

For a few years the Goffs could breathe a little easier financially. Shortly after Sherry's father died, Barclay's dad passed away, too, leaving his son enough money to buy a tiny cabin on a northern Michigan lake. They now owned a second home, all 642 square feet of it.

Barclay had switched jobs from the lumberyard chain twelve years earlier. After seventeen years in management there, he had moved over to become a manufacturer's rep—a traveling salesman—for a window company. He traveled around the state, using the cabin as a base for overnight stops when he was in the north. He discovered that he liked that part of his job, being on the road, meeting new people, listening to his conservative talk radio.

But a couple of years after Sherry started her job as an OT, Barclay's company reorganized and he was suddenly unemployed. The family became completely dependent on Sherry's salary of about forty thousand dollars. The gamble they had taken and the sacrifices they had made to send Sherry back to college were now proving their worth. Sherry's income had to cover their living expenses as well as Norah's, Molly's, and Sherry's college loans. Barclay immediately looked for work, but nothing lasted. He had about eight different temporary jobs in one year. He got his real estate license, which he thought he would use in finding vacation property to sell. But for about eighteen months Sherry was "the major breadwinner," Barclay was "the minor breadwinner," as she put it. Who knows how they would have coped if she hadn't had her job?

It's difficult for a salesman in his fifties to find a new job, and it was some time before Barclay saw the ad in the local paper for the National Write Your Congressman organization. National Write Your Congressman, a self-described nonpartisan, legislative research organization for businesses and professionals, is a kind of umbrella lobbying outfit that keeps its subscribers up to date on the voting history and issues before the U.S. Congress. Barclay liked the sound of it. The hours he had spent listening to conservative talk radio didn't just affect his politics. His commitment to his religion intensi- fied, as did his desire to serve. "It's a very Christian organization," said Barclay. "Which is good, because it requires a lot of faith, as you get turned down a lot of times. It's a very high turnover job. There are very few people who make it past the first year, because you have to deal with so much rejection. You don't have to have too many suc- cesses to make it financially, but you have to deal with eight to ten re- jections for every success."

Barclay loved his new job. He had found something to do that synthesizes his interests and his aptitude. He got to be a salesman again, which he loved and was clearly good at. He also got to feel that he was making a difference working for an organization that re- flected both his religious and his political views. Yet, as he pointed out, "Basically every Monday morning I am unemployed."

Each week, he'd begin again, getting in the car to go off selling packages for the National Write Your Congressman membership or- ganization. He described himself as an "independent contractor'" on straight commission. He made a decent living, but because of the hand-to-mouth nature of Barclay's income, the Goffs were depend- ent on Sherry's job for their stability and their benefits. It was the day-care situation in reverse. Only with more money coming in.

Sherry was making her own difference in her new career. I talked with one mother of an autistic son who had worked with her. The little boy had begun having problems at two and had been formally diagnosed when he was three years old.

What sets her apart from the other OTs is the way she works with the parents. Half the time, if you even give an idea you are blown off, because you are not an expert in that field. She is just so open to all that stuff . . . She got him writing. I never thought he would write. She just started with little tweezer things and very gradually got him to a pencil, and he writes whole paragraphs now in second grade. She was so patient with him . . . You don't have to question her. Usually I peek in with therapists, but I trusted her.

Hannah Goff left for college—with her scholarships—in the fall of 2007. The Goff parents remained at home with their dog, finally empty nesters. Both continued to work hard. They would be paying off college loans for some time. Barclay dreamed of being able to take his wife on a round-the-world cruise one day. Sherry looked forward to a time when she might be able to cut back to a four-day week.

Meanwhile, she took Gracie for walks, taught Bible studies at church, visited regularly with her mother, talked daily with her daughters, enjoyed her time with her friends, relaxed at the cabin with her husband, and each day made an enormous difference in the lives of a number of young children in her community.

Lauren Jacobson

Ubuntu ungamntu ngabanye abantu.
Xhosa saying—*A person becomes a person through
other people.*

THE IDEA THAT the course of a life can be changed by a single water-shed event is not new or uncommon. You happen to be in the right place at the right time—or the wrong place at the wrong time—and something happens that takes you off the road you were following so comfortably and sets you on an entirely different course.

E. B. White even introduced this idea to children in his book *The Trumpet of the Swan.* "In almost everyone's life there is one event that changes the whole course of his existence," he wrote as Sam Beaver entered the Philadelphia Zoo and decided he wanted to be a zookeeper. But some of these turning points don't always take place in such quiet moments. Sometimes they stand out because they are dramatic. Your life flows toward a crisis with its own momentum, and only later do you look back and understand why crisis means change. Lauren Jacobson and her family experienced such a dramatic event in 1997. A violent attack in Johannesburg picked them up out of the life they had been living and put them down half a world away, forcing Lauren to redefine who she was and what her priorities were.

I first heard of Lauren when I lived in South Africa in the early 1990s. Perhaps I met her once or twice, but I think I would have remembered her if I did. Our worlds overlapped, but we didn't connect. I was there for a short time as a journalist, doing freelance features and then concentrating solely on the story of Winnie Mandela. Lauren was a partner in one of the country's most prestigious law firms, concentrating on human rights cases and media law.

Our professional lives intertwined when Winnie Mandela and her soccer team were suspects in a murder, and Lauren represented the victim's family. Eventually my publisher hired her to read my biography for libel. I knew *of* Lauren for a long time before I actually knew her. In fact, I found her intimidating. She had such an impressive reputation, I thought she must be at least a decade older than me. It was only when I began interviewing her for this book that I learned how much older she really is—one day.

Growing up at the same time but a world away from me, Lauren was one of five children (she was the second) who grew up to the sound of their mother typing her dissertation as she worked on her master's degree in speech therapy. At the time, this achievement in South Africa was unusual enough for a woman of her background to get a headline in the local paper ("Master Mum Is Mother of 5!"). "She is," observed her daughter, "a tenacious woman." If Lauren got her tenacity from her mother, she got her love of law from her father, himself a lawyer who worked just hard enough to finish his workday in time to come home for dinner with his family.

The Jacobson household was lively but chaotic. Hopeless at getting anywhere on time, when they went places the family often mistakenly left a child behind without realizing it. "My father would turn to the backseat of the station wagon, and there would invariably be a child missing." Sometimes the child was Lauren, as she lost herself in books on the beach. Once, the police brought her back to the holiday apartment after dark. Another time, "We were visiting family friends in another town and I snuck away to read. My family left without me, and only when my dad asked for a show of hands halfway home did they realize." Childhood dinners consisted of high-volume debates about politics or literature accompanied by relentless teasing. Lauren had one sister but three brothers and four first cousins—all boys. But as one of the oldest she was well able to hold her own.

As a teenager she was sent to what she described as "a helpful feminine refuge." Pretoria High School for Girls, a government high school that was politically liberal but socially conservative, had been modeled on the girls' schools of England. Students wore uniforms, with berets in winter and panamas in summer. There was not one male on the premises—that Lauren could remember, no members of staff, not even the gardener. The absence of boys—or the absence of having to worry about playing to boys—made the girls less self-conscious about being bookish. As a result, they tended to become ambitious, do well academically, and go on to college and solid careers.

Like many of her classmates, Lauren went to Wits University (University of the Witwatersrand), South Africa's best, where she got two degrees—one in arts and one in law. She accomplished both degrees in the minimum amount of time, five years, then went straight to Bell Dewar Hall as an article clerk. Two years after she qualified to practice she was made the firm's first woman partner. It sounds impressive and it is. But to keep a sense of perspective about Lauren's success as a lawyer in South Africa, it helps to remember what a small world she lived in. Which is not to say she isn't an extremely bright, energetic, and capable woman, but there just weren't many others like her.

At Bell Dewar Hall Lauren very quickly zeroed in on human rights issues. "I always wanted to do it. It seemed to me at that time in South Africa to be in possession of a law degree and not use it in the public interest just seemed inconceivable."

In that particular time and place, working in the public interest

meant dealing with cases involving detention without trial, specifically with the abuses that can take place when detainees are never
brought to trial. The issues were not dissimilar to those twenty years
later of Guantánamo Bay. As a young lawyer, Lauren visited detainees in prison and documented their conditions. She then tried to
improve those conditions, by preventing torture or bringing in food,
medicine, or books. Almost every step she took on behalf of her
clients involved an additional—or parallel—step to court.

The government had declared a national state of emergency,
"Which is tantamount to declaring war upon yourself—it's a form of
civil war," Lauren explained. "And you [the government] say that as
part of the fight you have to be able to act in ways that are not, generally speaking, lawful in terms of both domestic and international
law . . . With each test case to bring in food or money or reading material, bit by bit we created little breathing holes into what was a
blanket clampdown." Which is not to say that all of her clients saw
her as their savior. Many, particularly the younger and more politically extreme men, were not especially thrilled to have a white woman
represent them. "It wasn't all mutual respect and gratification and
gratitude," she pointed out. More than once she felt antipathy from
both sides in the struggle.

In 1989, at the age of twenty-eight, Lauren's professional and personal worlds turned upside down. First she met Keith Coleman at a
party. She already knew his parents. Max and Audrey Coleman were
well-known activists with whom she used to consult regularly on
her detainee work. Keith and Lauren had a lot in common. He had
devoted his life to challenging the apartheid system, motivated by a
desire to empower the country's black population. As a sixteen-year-
old student at a progressive liberal school in Johannesburg, he became involved in the political resistance following the 1976 Soweto
student uprising. A year later he joined the student movement at
Wits University, eventually being named chairman of the student
African movement.

In 1979 he created a student newspaper that was officially intended solely for white campuses. Secretly, it was also distributed to townships and trade unions. The paper was quickly banned and the offices firebombed. In October 1981 Keith was arrested and detained for five months before being banned for two years.* His banning order expired in 1984, but in 1985, when the South African government declared a state of emergency, Keith went underground and lived in hiding for two years.

By the time he resurfaced in 1988, he was running an organization that provided training and education for unions, women's groups, youth groups, and student groups. He would run education sessions under the cover of road bridges to hide from helicopters. He wrote a book on how to negotiate for a living wage. A number of his colleagues were detained and killed. And shortly after he came out of hiding, his offices were bombed.

In 1989, the year that he met Lauren, the country was looking forward to a new future. In preparation, Keith went back to Wits University to get an MBA and then wrote a book on nationalization. The following year he joined the African National Congress's Department of Economic Policy. Then he joined a management consulting firm and started advising the new government from the outside. There was a lot to do—roads to be built, electricity to be connected, water pipes to be laid. For someone of Keith's background, it was an invigorating time of hope and hard work.

Keith and Lauren decided very quickly to get married. "I'm so bloody impulsive," she said. She saw herself as an "old-fashioned girl" who knew she wanted children, but the decision probably had a lot to

---

* Banning orders typically restricted an individual to one magisterial district, required them to report regularly to the police, and prevented them from associating with more than one person at any time (including family members). They could not visit various public places or educational institutions. Additionally, nothing the banned person said or wrote could be quoted in the press or used for publication. There was no avenue for appeal against a banning order.

do with her wanting a secure and loving home to go to work from. The year she met Keith her professional life became more treacherous. She had taken on two similar cases, both assassinations—one of a white man, the other an Indian, both activists. The bigger case actually came to her second. On May 1, a national holiday, she and Keith were woken by a phone call telling of the assassination of David Webster. Webster was an old friend of Keith's, as well as an old foe of the government in Pretoria. He had been shot in front of his girlfriend a mile or two away.

Such an assassination automatically triggered an official inquest, which was not necessarily the same thing as an impartial or honest inquiry. To get at the truth, families of the deceased would often hire their own legal representatives as "watching briefs." A watching brief would have the authority to shadow and monitor official justice process. Webster's surviving partner, Maggie Friedman, hired Lauren to be her watching brief. The investigation eventually broadened into an inquest that led to the exposé of South Africa's death squads—the existence of the country's so-called third force, a secret organization composed of elements from both the army and the police, who were dedicated to preventing change in the South African way of life. After three former police officers announced in late 1989 that they had been members of an officially authorized and funded police death squad known as the Civil Co-operation Bureau, or CCB, stories about hit squads made national and international news.

As the official representative of the Webster estate, Lauren continued to take death squad testimony from soldiers in exile and from convicts or arrestees hoping to cut a deal by telling what they knew. "It was very scary, very stressful," she said. "I felt very vulnerable as a woman."

All the environments in which she worked—the police, the courts, the Harms Commission (set up by President F. W. de Klerk's government to investigate the allegations)—were male dominated. Not just male, but white Afrikaans male. Women had their place in this world, and it was not across a desk or in a courtroom. Lauren was pigeonholed before she even spoke. She was young, she was female, and she cared about the way she looked. In the mornings as she got ready for work, she never knew what to wear. Should she dress down and dowdy to avoid attention?

Any woman who has ever experienced sexism or sexual harassment can relate to that uncomfortable aspect of Lauren's job. But add to the mix—or to the discomfort—a fear of physical danger, and the stress multiplies. Lauren never stopped wondering what she would do if "they" came for her. She had no strength or training to match what might come her way.

The Harms Commission (so named because it sat under the jurisdiction of judge Louis Harms) met in both Pretoria and London for two years. Lauren traveled regularly to both places to question witnesses before the commission. To any outsider she appeared capable and confident. "I saw her proudly standing up there and doing her number," said John Carlin, who covered South Africa for the *London Independent* and became a close friend of Lauren's during this time. "She was very brave—pronouncing on the nature of white South Africans . . . I think she was pretty unique. At this level it was a man's world."

Eventually the Harms Commission issued a report that found—nothing. It didn't name anyone responsible for Webster's death or pinpoint anyone behind any of the acts alleged to have been committed by the "third force." In all there were seven investigations into Webster's death, all of which Lauren participated in. Not one uncovered his killers.

At the same time, she had been hired to be the watching brief on another killing. The alleged mastermind behind this murder was not from the white government but from the other side. The victim was Dr. Abu-Baker Asvat, and the woman who had much to gain from his death was Winnie Mandela. Dr. Asvat, who was of Indian descent, had a small general practice office in Soweto, where he served the people of the township with the help of his well-respected nurse, Albertina Sisulu, the wife of Nelson Mandela's trusted friend Walter Sisulu. Asvat had been shot to death in his office in late January 1989 by two youths. One of the youths implicated Winnie in his statement to the police when he was arrested.

This was another story that reverberated around the world. At the heart of this case was Winnie Mandela's "soccer team," Mandela United. The irony, apparent to many, was that the actions of Mandela United and the actions of the third force were remarkably similar.*

During the investigation of both assassinations, South Africa changed radically. The African National Congress was reinstated, Nelson Mandela was released from jail, and the country prepared for its first democratic elections.

It was an exciting time, yet there was a demoralizing *new* fear. Violent crime began almost exactly as apartheid ended. "The fear was supposed to have been lifted," said Lauren. "Political change came, and I think it was replaced by another kind of fear. There was supposed to be relief and I thought—selfishly—that the new country was going to be an easier place for me to live in. And it wasn't."

She craved some kind of recognition from her family and peers that her work was treacherous and her life unsafe. But in South Africa her fears and experiences didn't really rate, so she never got

---

* To briefly summarize the facts of the second inquest: Asvat had been consulted by his close friend Winnie—and had the records with time and date stamps to prove it—in the kidnapping and assault of a number of local boys by Mandela United. One of the kidnapped boys—Stompie Seipei—had been murdered. Winnie's associate and the "coach" of Mandela United was subsequently found guilty of Stompie's killing. Winnie herself was eventually brought to trial on charges of kidnapping and assault and found guilty of ordering the kidnapping. (She was acquitted of the assault after she produced an alibi saying she was out of town on the days in question. The alibi was never investigated or challenged by the police or the prosecution.)

Asvat had gone to Winnie's house to examine the boys after their assault—an experience he had found shocking. He immediately described what he had seen to community leaders in an attempt to secure the boys' release. He was murdered the next day.

The Asvat family initially thought that right-wing forces had killed Abu, which was why they hired Lauren. Asvat had been politically active and a member of the extreme group Black Consciousness.

the acknowledgment nor the support that she needed. "If you compare people on Robben Island who had been tortured to death in prison to a middle-class white woman who is going out to parties on a Saturday night and buying designer clothes, you just don't have the right to complain."

When you read about countries across the world in states of "domestic upheaval," you don't really get a sense of the daily impact of constant fear. I had a taste of it when I was researching my biography of Winnie Mandela. No one threatened me personally, and I was never attacked. But people let me know that I was being noticed, and that's all it took. Every time I turned the key in my car, I braced myself for an explosion that never came. I would walk into my house or wake up in the night, listening for the sounds of nonexistent intruders. I hid my notes as well as I could but never felt they were safe, so I took to sending them out of the country.

Being afraid is like having a kind of lingering virus. You never feel quite well. Lauren used to feel the fear literally lift from her as the wheels of her plane took off the runway on a flight to London. I felt the same sense of relief. But like Lauren, I felt the fear was something I had to overcome. I couldn't give in to it and neither could she. When you work in that kind of climate—or when your work causes that kind of climate—your job becomes extremely precious. You become even more conscientious, more thorough, more tenacious. You don't necessarily feel brave; in fact, you're scared, and you know that you are more vulnerable because you are a woman. The threat of rape is real. But both Lauren and I felt proud that we were able to continue working in our different fields despite being women.

Lauren was twenty-nine when she married Keith in May 1990. As South Africa entered the nineties and Lauren crossed into her thirties, the urgent court applications of yesterday became the media and entertainment deals of today. Shortly after her wedding, she decided to make a break with the prestigious, clubby, Bell Dewar Hall and set up her own firm with two young partners. This led to the creation of Jacobson, Rosin & Wright. Rather than taking offices close to the other law firms and businesses in an increasingly dangerous downtown Johannesburg, they chose to buy a large, attractive house in the northern suburbs, close to where she and her fellow partners lived.

At the time of that decision she was pregnant with her first son, Miles. Overall she was leading a more normal life. She was working in a professional, not a criminal, environment. She was happily married. And her focus had begun to shift to the balance of work and family. "For us it had a lot to do with convenience," she said, explaining why she chose to put her offices in a house rather than an office building. "A number of our clients were women with children; maybe they would like to bring them if that was the only time we could have a meeting. We would like to be able to bring our own children if we needed to, to an environment where they could play, do their homework. It was about as easy as juggling work and family gets. It was perfect in many ways."

What she created was a place that any professional woman might envy. No cubicles or long corridors to tiptoe down, but a big garden and a proper kitchen for children and their working parents to enjoy. The office was a ten-minute drive from the local preschool and not much farther from her house. Once Miles started school, she could easily go and fetch him for lunch. The environment was relaxed, comfortable—and safe.

In a law firm in a country where television licenses were about to be awarded for the first time, where the media business was about to explode, the founding partner of a new niche law firm couldn't think about taking off too much time for maternity leave. So she didn't. Lauren took phone calls almost from the moment she gave birth and was reengaged in legal matters after only a couple of weeks. She was back at work full-time when Miles was six weeks old. Part of her desire to return to the firm was that her work was fun, but part of it was that all of her friends worked and there was no one to hang out with at home. This was not a stay-at-home crowd. When she left Bell Dewar, her office consisted of a room in her in-laws' home—then she rented temporary office space nearby and was able to breast-feed her baby until he was nine months old.

Potential clients knew who she was. She had an outstanding reputation in a confined world where social and professional lives tended to overlap. In the South Africa of the eighties and nineties "networking" was a Saturday night activity. "I don't think we had any friends who were in business; everyone we knew was in the media or the arts or were consultants in government devising new economic plans for post-apartheid South Africa. It was a very vibrant group of people," said Lauren.

The vibrant friends could also send work her way, which was a plus in setting up a small law firm.

> We were three lawyers and a fax machine. We had no way of knowing [whether or not this would work]. We didn't test, there was no market research, and the ethics of the profession prevent you from touting clients, so we couldn't ask, "If we were to do this, would you come?" We had to take a massive leap of faith that our instincts were right, so that even if existing clients didn't come with us, we would get new clients. The very first within a day of unpacking our little pencil cases in Audrey and Max's house, AP phoned with an urgent application and we had our first big case.

Within weeks, they had clients such as ABC News and ITN. After that they represented the first new television license consortium. They got the Classic FM radio station into South Africa. They handled film work when production companies flocked to shoot films cheaply in the country. They represented both the old local newspapers and new publications. And they worked with the new government, taking part in a task force that was drafting new legislation from scratch on gambling as well as setting up a new broadcasting complaints commission.

It was clear to everyone, both inside and outside the firm, who the driving force was. "There is a side to Lauren, she knows what she wants," said Claire Wright, who became the third partner and was only two years younger. "Lauren doesn't do soul searching. She doesn't work out what other people want from her. It can be wonderful and frustrating for people working with her. She is doing it on her terms." Everyone consulted Lauren. She became the go-to lawyer for any kind of media issue. That's why my publishers chose her to read my biography on Winnie Mandela. My husband, Bill, quoted her in a *New York Times* article on press freedom

For a few years life ticked along. Keith was busy with the new government; Lauren had lots of business, one baby, then two. Miles was now at preschool, and Lauren could go and get him for lunch at the office in the middle of the day. A faint cloud appeared on the horizon when Sam was about eight months old and had a seizure. It was a frightening episode, but there was nothing to suggest it might not have been caused by anything more sinister than a fever or a virus. The rhythm of the Coleman life was secure—until January 1997.

The day began—as they often do—with no hint of what was to come, in the calmest, most ordinary of ways. It was a sunny Sunday morning in Johannesburg. Lauren and Keith were taking their two sons, Miles, now four, and Sam, almost one, to a Sunday barbeque at their friends Jim Smith and Maxine Hart's house.

January is summer in South Africa, a time of year when the white middle-class population of Johannesburg likes to barbeque. Sundays are often spent in the back gardens of suburban homes, next to pools or on patios, surrounded by scented bushes that bloom abundantly behind high walls, electric fences, and elaborate security systems. The Smith-Harts and their new baby boy lived in one such pretty detached suburban home. Like everyone else they knew, they had an electric gate. They enjoyed a life of relative affluence set against a climate of increasing fear. In some ways it was the ideal environment to raise a child. There was plenty of space, nice weather, good schools. But by this day in early 1997 the residential areas of South Africa were increasingly described as gilded cages. The sun might have been shining, but the atmosphere was brooding.

Nelson Mandela had been president of South Africa for almost three years, and the "new" South Africa had acquired a familiarity. Blacks and whites could now live and work together. The country was governed by a majority of blacks. *Oppression* was a word from the past. Mandela himself had said in his inaugural address, "Never, never and never again shall it be that this beautiful land will again experience the oppression of one by another." But there was a new and uncomfortable oppression, particularly in suburban Johannesburg, spoken of in hushed voices and not dwelt on by its victims. It shattered lives and dreams and caused many to flee. The new oppression was crime. And, increasingly, its target was the white middle class. Black South Africans had been victims of township violence for decades. Now the white minority began to share their experience.

South African crime in the 1990s was terrifyingly violent, and its biracial element was new. In 1998, the same year that a BBC report described Johannesburg as the "epicenter" of South African crime, Interpol recorded that South Africa had the highest recorded per capita murder rate in the world. That year, the Crime Information Analysis Center of the South African police force reported that a serious crime was committed in South Africa every seventeen seconds. One in twenty families was the victim of robbery with aggravated circumstances. It was those "aggravated circumstances" that chilled. Pets were killed, women were raped in front of their children, children were tied up in closets, and men were shot dead. A robbery often didn't last seconds or minutes, but all night long, as a gang of thugs got personal with a family. Carjackings were the most common crime, and they usually took place in people's driveways. Carjackings were frequently accompanied by another act of violence. If you were held up at gunpoint and ordered out of your car, you'd most likely be shot before the robber drove off.

Like many of her friends, Lauren had been living in fear for months. When she and Keith went out on Saturday nights, she would panic on their return home. "There was always this heart-stopping moment: Is everything okay? Not just the obvious—Has one of them had a fever? Or, has one of them been crying? But, are they all still alive in there?"

Jim Smith was the Colemans' host at the Sunday barbeque. He explained their arrival this way:

> We had them around, as you do. It was just going to be them. Our house overlooked across the street a golf course. What should be a benign and enticing view of South Africa becomes ominous. People can hide there. We had an eight-foot-tall fence and sliding electric gates. You get out of your car and there is a buzzer. They rang the buzzer and it opens and slides across quite slowly, as these gates do—they are open for a certain amount of time. The gate buzzed open, and Keith, who was driving, slowly pulled forward into the driveway. Then he saw the gunmen. He said, "Oh no." One of the guys pointed a gun at his head and said, "Oh yes."

Smith recalled opening the front door absentmindedly and taking a minute to realize what was going on.

> Keith and Lauren are coming up the stairs. And as they are coming up, they are coming up with a guy with a gun. You could see on their faces shock more than terror. And the dogs are barking and the gunman is there, and we are standing on the front steps of our house. And then there is another gunman coming up, and they are on the doorstep and the dogs start

barking hysterically, and the gunman is pointing at the dogs and threatening to shoot the dogs. Somehow we quieted the dogs. I remember Maxine was standing at the door and she was breast-feeding our then-four-month-old, Daniel. And the guys come in with what I remember to be nine-millimeter pistols. They are standing in the entry hall, and I remember raising my hand, trying to be calm and saying, "We're peaceful people, just don't hurt anybody. Take what you need to take."

Maxine remembered the guy saying, "Yeah, we're peaceful, too."

Lauren had come into the house with her older son, four-year-old Miles. But contrary to what Smith remembered, Keith had not come up the stairs behind her. He was out in the driveway with his car and two more gunmen, trying to negotiate. Why? His baby, Sam, was still strapped into the car seat in the back, and Keith was terrified he would be driven off in the car. He was doing his best to get permission to remove his son before the car was taken.

"There was one guy who was completely wired," said Keith.

He was extremely nervous, he kept waving his gun around my face; he must have been stoned or something. He was really twitchy. There was another guy who was much calmer. And I just blotted the twitchy guy out of my consciousness, and I just looked at this other guy who was their leader and negotiated with him to get Sam out of that car. It was absolutely in total slow motion that it all happened. And getting Sam out of the car and getting these guys out of the house were the only things I had in my mind.

But it was very tense, because they thought I had a gun in Sam's car seat. So the twitchy guy, when I started to reach in to get Sam, very slowly, he pulled me back, and then he just felt all around Sam's car seat. And he unclipped Sam from his belt and felt behind Sam. I eventually got Sam out. That was phase one completed. I now had Sam in my arms. Stage two was to focus on Miles and Lauren.

Inside the house, Maxine was walking around looking for money while breast-feeding. Lauren handed over her watch with no idea what was happening outside to her husband and baby. She knew all the scenarios. She began to plan for what she thought would be her inevitable rape in front of her small son, thinking of ways she could pretend it was all a game.

But as many people told her afterward, in the ham-handed comforting remarks of the well-meaning, she was lucky. Suddenly it was over. Once Sam was out of the car, the gunmen got into it and drove off. The wives were not violated; the men were not beaten up or shot. No one died. Within half an hour the Colemans had even got their car back—found just a few blocks away. By the standards of the day the victims had had a *lucky escape.*

When they returned home that afternoon they were a different family. For years Lauren had lived with the fear that *she* might suffer some kind of personal attack. She had lived with fear long before she became a mother. By the time she had children, her professional situation had changed and she no longer felt she was a specific target. Yet at the same time as she personally became safer, the situation within South Africa as a whole changed, and women—mothers— became general targets. She *and her children* had been attacked. As she said, it might easily happen again. Next time they might not be as lucky. Her reaction was immediate. She had to get her kids out of there. She had to flee to protect them. "As these guys who attacked us drove off, I watched them. And as I watched them drive off, I said to Keith, 'We're out of here.' And those were the first words I spoke to him after the attack. It was utterly instinctive, and part of my instinct was that *statistics have no memory.*"

Six weeks later the Colemans were on a plane to London. They went quickly, as Lauren put it "impulsively," leaving behind their house, their friends, their family, and—though they didn't realize it at the time—Lauren's career. Neither of them knew how long they would be away, but surely neither of them expected that they would never return to South Africa to live. Both of them wanted to clear their heads and feel safe. They both agreed that the trauma of the event could be turned into an impetus to try to live somewhere else for a while.

Before they left they went to see a trauma counselor, who pointed out that the experience had highlighted the strength of their marriage. The couple had coped as a team, communicating instinctively with an effective, albeit unspoken, strategy of dividing the responsibility of the children. The counselor emphasized that the Colemans had had no choice but to comply with their attackers. Her emphasis made Keith and Lauren feel less powerless, yet the degree was relative. They saw the world differently now. Their fear of being victims was based on experience. "I would have given in to and accepted what had happened to us if I could have traded it for a promise of it never happening again," said Lauren. "But the incidence of crime was such that there was a very good chance that it *would* happen again."

Lauren Jacobson is not a cowardly woman. Before this incident, her life and work had been full of many heart-stopping moments, all caused by choices she had made as she and her husband solidly worked toward ending apartheid and creating a more egalitarian society.

But what about her husband? He's no coward, either. For years Lauren suffered from guilt, believing she had forced Keith to leave South Africa at a time when he was involved and invested in creating utopia. As she put it, "I needed to heal by leaving; he needed to heal by staying." She didn't find out for many years that he was as keen to go as she was. He, too, felt devastated by the attack—for the same reasons.

I realized that I had survived detention and life banning and attempts on my life in a political world, and none of that had driven me out of the country. And then there were these four—or five—young criminals who in twenty minutes just destroyed my future in the country. And there was no way I could justify living there . . . When it happened, all my assumptions about my life and my future collapsed. I had to recognize very rapidly that I had to leave *in order to protect my family*. It was an instant realization, and I instantly came to terms with it in terms of reality . . . Emotionally I am still coming to terms with it.

Many women stop work when they and their families relocate. Some quit to focus on their kids after a traumatic event. Some wives give up careers because their husbands have impossible schedules. And some mothers, as we've already seen with Judith Feder, decide to stay at home when they have a child with problems. Lauren fit into all of the above categories.

Sam had had another seizure just after the attack in Johannesburg, making his parents wonder whether he was having some reaction to the trauma. Then he had another one. Clearly something was the matter and he needed help. When the Colemans arrived in London—a city where they were complete strangers—in the spring of 1997, Lauren had to pick a neighborhood, look for a house, find a school for Miles and doctors for Sam. She had to do all of this with no help and without knowing her way round. "When I look back to those times, getting the name of the doctor was easy; *finding* the doctor was another story."

There was no question of working. All of these were full-time assignments. She wasn't on the Internet yet. And the Web sites that now exist to help with searches were in their infancy. Sam's health was the priority. She started from scratch, with a friend who was related to a pediatrician in London. Slowly and methodically, using all the energy and resourcefulness that had made her so successful professionally, Lauren found her son medical help. Then as Sam grew, developed, and improved, she found him therapeutic help, followed by supplemental educational help. Over the years, his condition and prognosis got stronger and stronger. He shone in some areas—his reading and vocabulary skills were outstanding, and he had extraordinary musical gifts. He still struggled in others, especially in the area of social skills. By the time he was ten, he was in a mainstream state school in North London, getting extra help where he needed it but easily keeping up academically.

However difficult the logistics of resettling might have been—and they were clearly overwhelming—there was one huge advantage to this new life: it was a life without fear. Lauren felt almost carefree as she adjusted to not being scared. She took tremendous pleasure from being able to walk down the street, open the windows of her house, or pick up a bottle of milk from the doorstep. Her life was in a state of crisis. Yet for the first time in decades she felt safe.

There were mundane things, like this house had sash windows that led straight onto a road, and I could open them, and I could forget to close them, and it would be absolutely fine. It was a front door with an ordinary Yale lock. I didn't have to navigate gates and fences and activate alarms. And walking down the street with the children. The fact that I *did walk* down the street. The fact that I didn't have a car or need a car because I felt perfectly safe walking places with them and doing things with them. When Keith started to travel and commute, I didn't feel anxious at night. I didn't have sleepless nights listening for noises. Everything was so difficult, so demanding here, but at the same time I remember having moments of just complete joy, like the fact that milk got delivered (a) because the milkman can actually get up your front stairs as opposed to [having to] deactivate your alarm and your electric fence, and (b) nobody stole it.

She found a house on a Hampstead street where she discovered she was surrounded by fellow transplants, even some South

Africans. In a city, a *country,* not especially known for its hospitality to strangers, the new arrivals found themselves in a community of generous-spirited neighbors, who recommended shops, amenities, and schools.

Meanwhile, Keith was commuting to and from South Africa. At the time of their departure, he was employed by the Boston-based political consulting firm Monitor to work in South Africa. Monitor agreed that he could move to London and continue to work in South Africa from there. The company paid for the move and provided temporary housing for the family on their arrival.

For three years Keith flew out to South Africa on a Sunday night and returned to London the following Friday. He went straight to work in Johannesburg from the plane on Monday morning. After ten days he'd fly back to London to spend ten days with his family, working from home before heading out again. It was a tough routine, similar to the one Warren Feder had followed five years earlier shortly after his twins were born. As was the case with the Feders, this was a difficult time for a husband and father to be away from his family. Many choices that families face involve sacrifice. In both of these situations the fathers had to choose what to give up. There were times when Keith might have thought he was giving it all up. He felt disconnected from his wife and children, disconnected from the country he was settling into, disconnected from the one he was working in, and he was exhausted.

What choice had he had? The Colemans' primary desire was to leave their home quickly. That meant Lauren had to stop working. But Keith couldn't. It made no sense to arrive in a new and expensive country with no work at all. Keith might not have had much time with his family, but he could take comfort in the fact that he was supporting them. Besides, leaving South Africa and its struggles had been a very difficult psychological move for him. The slow transition made the departure easier. For three years he was still making a difference.

I would just work eighteen hours a day. I would live in a hotel, and it was actually quite nice because I didn't actually *leave* South Africa. I carried on working. I missed Lauren and the kids a lot, and it was very hard for Lauren, too; she had to create the home. It was a very, very tough period for her. London is a majorly expensive city, so we didn't have too many options that were affordable . . . so I just did it. It was nice to continue working there. The travel was brutal. One year I did twenty-six flights.

Many women who stop working have to adjust to having more time on their hands. Lauren had less. She was constantly rushing. She had very little help—none at all at the beginning, then the occasional babysitter she would hire by the hour. Several times a week she had to collect Miles from school and then get across London with her two boys for Sam to have doctor's appointments and tests.

It's possible to be racing through a day as fast as you can and still be lonely. Lauren missed Keith. "Especially those interminable Sundays that start at six a.m. with two small kids to keep entertained. I remember heading with them to a park in Keith's baggy tracksuit pants, feeling wrecked, only to bump into an immaculately groomed woman from my past looking fresh as a daisy, taking turns with her husband to push their kid in the swing."

Because she was on her own so much, Lauren was motivated to socialize and build a new network of friends. But while she was setting up her new life, she had to dismantle her old one. As they had boarded the flight for London, they left with the thought that they might be gone for a year. It was soon clear as they settled down that a year wouldn't be enough time. As the months passed, they made decisions that took them further and further away from a return to South Africa. They sold their house in Johannesburg. Before she had left, Lauren told her two partners she was going immediately without giving them any notice. Soon it became clear she wasn't coming back.

Lauren was offered a few jobs when she first got to London, including a senior position at the Disney Company. She remembered, "I decided that the commute (North London to Hammersmith) and the fact that it was a full-time job made it a non-starter. The kids were small, we were barely settled here, and Keith was commuting to S.A., et cetera, et cetera."

Lauren might have been all consumed with taking care of her family, but how did they afford to have her not work? They had moved from a relatively inexpensive country where they both worked to one of the most expensive cities in the world with only one income. Lauren pointed out that they "didn't come over as paupers." They used savings to put down a small deposit on a house. But they were largely able to maintain their lifestyle because of Keith's job. The London office of the Monitor group not only agreed to move Keith to London, but they also provided him with a number of fairly generous benefits over and above the temporary housing. They paid for all the moving costs, including moving the family car. (The one that had been hijacked and recovered ended up being like a member of the family, going with them to London.) They covered all of Keith's travel expenses to and from South Africa. And they adjusted his salary to London standards, which represented a significant increase. The Colemans might have had numerous problems, but money wasn't one of them. In fact, they were doing well enough to send Miles to private school.

Which is not to say they didn't worry. By the time they sold their South African house, the property market had plummeted—not surprisingly, given the level of crime—and they "had to give it away," as Lauren put it. They sold one house at the bottom of the market as they bought their next one at the top.

They had no family support to help with child care, as they did in Johannesburg, and professional help was extremely expensive. This was an issue because Sam had doctor's appointments at difficult times in inconvenient places. In the early days Lauren arranged his

schedule so that she could get back to Hampstead in time to pick
Miles up from school. Eventually she hired a nursery school teacher
to help with Miles after school on an hourly as-needed basis. Still, as
Lauren described it, it was "a very, very, very, very long time" before
she felt able to think about work. "It was a long time before I felt like
I wanted to or felt I could do anything other than keep things afloat."

When she did feel a little more relaxed, two years after she'd first
arrived in England, she decided to revisit a love of drama she'd had
since school and took a screenwriting course at Birkbeck College,
part of London University. It wasn't an arduous program. The class
met once a week for a year. After that she attended a local creative
writing course run by a neighbor, and she began to do some occasional freelance legal consulting for those who were sent her way by
former clients in South Africa. Then she tried out her entrepreneurial skills. With some friends she organized a London exhibition and
sale of crafts from South Africa. It was never intended to be a proper
business, but it made her realize that she wanted to go back to work.
Her question was, What could she do next? She didn't want to work
in a law firm; she didn't know if she *could* work in one in London.
She knew she had to do *something*. She had exhausted the excitement and novelty of being in London. Unlike Johannesburg, London is a city where many mothers don't work, but Lauren had
reached the point where "it was like how many times can we do lunch
or coffee?"

By now Keith had left the Monitor group and had set up his own
consulting business. At the end of each day, Lauren would beg him
for what she called "news from the front" to get some kind of a
sense of life in the real world.

I found myself just pounding poor Keith for information as he
walked in the front door. About anything he had done at work.
I think in many ways it was very nice for him and very good for
our marriage, because I would engage with what he was doing

at work, because I desperately needed the stimulation. And we would have these long discussions about problems at work, and sometimes there were even legal problems, in which case it was particularly exciting. And I realized that the way I was talking through the stuff with him was pathological.

This was not a life she had imagined for herself.

That's when I compared myself with women who seemed utterly content with life, and I realized they were pretty much living out their aspirations, whereas I was living something that was so far removed from what I had imagined for myself that I was having real difficulty. More difficulty in a lot of ways than the early months in London, where life had thrown some curved balls, so you deal. It's very different from [having] settled into some kind of rhythm.

She felt like she was settling into a groove that she didn't like. And she began to experience self-doubt. *"The more time that went by the more panicky I got about what I could possibly do."*
All of that fear she had lived with for so long had never once undermined her confidence in her professional abilities. But time at home succeeded in being corrosive in a different way. Outsiders still saw her as a confident woman with a future, but now she found their confidence in her irritating. "Everybody kept saying to me, 'Of course you're going to get a job,' and I found that completely maddening as I kept thinking, What do you know? You don't know the first thing about me."
She had found a house, schools, medical treatment, domestic help, friends, courses to take, projects to work on. She had created a vibrant, happy life for everyone in her immediate family. Any outsider would imagine she could get herself any kind of work she chose. But when it came to reestablishing her career, she couldn't

imagine how she could possibly succeed. She had finally come to an obstacle she felt she couldn't climb.

So much fear, and then so much distraction for so many years, and now this paralysis. Imagine Lauren's frustration and panic as she looked to her future and saw—nothing. She had no professional network to help her. When she did meet the odd person (through Keith) who might have been interested in her résumé, she found their complete disinterest in her devastating. This enforced idleness seemed endless. As it turns out, it was little more than well-earned breathing space.

She began to think about teaching, because the British government was clearly as desperate for teachers as she was for a job. There was, as she put it, "this big missing space in my brain for work." She joined a book club. And to occupy her mind, she began to get more and more involved with Keith's work. They would sit together at home for hours, drafting things together and strategizing.

Keith once made the point that Lauren was "all about relationships." His wife, he said, was a woman "who put a relationship first." If a relationship was in place that she enjoyed, the chances were she would be able to turn it into something more. And it was through a friendship that Lauren ended up going back to work.

Keith had begun consulting at the Department of Constitutional Affairs (DCA), another name for the British Ministry of Justice. He had been lent the office of the department's constitution director, Andrew McDonald, while McDonald was away. When McDonald got back the two men temporarily shared the office space, got to know each other, and liked each other enough to arrange dinner with their wives. The dinner led to an invitation to McDonald's birthday picnic, on a hot summer's day in Kew Gardens.

"There was a lot of drinking of wine in the outdoors," said Lauren.

And I ended up having a long conversation with Andrew about the fact that there were these massive constitutional changes happening here, of which Andrew was in charge. And I remember having a bit of a conversation about freedom of information, but it kind of blurred with throwing balls to the children and other conversations with other people. And we were stumbling out of Kew Gardens much later, and I said to Keith, "I think Andrew offered me a job." And I really wasn't sure. Andrew had told me to ring his assistant, which I did with huge trepidation, and what it was—what it turned out to be—was that they were setting up a new supreme court here, which meant taking the law lords out of the House of Lords and setting up a freestanding supreme court.

The Labour Party manifesto for the 1997 election (the birth of "new Labour") had included proposals for a number of constitutional changes, from wresting power from the House of Lords to the creation of a Freedom of Information Act. Tony Blair pledged a wide-ranging review of both the reform of the civil justice system and legal aid.

When the Labour Party formed its government, the Department of Constitutional Affairs was charged with implementing the judicial changes. It was a big task that left its staff shorthanded. This was to Lauren's advantage. "I met Andrew at a time when he was casting around for people who could do this work at short notice and who ideally had had some kind of constitutional experience in another jurisdiction where there was a supreme court, and there I was."

McDonald saw a woman who was "clearly terribly bright and terribly able," who sounded pessimistic about finding something she could do in England. He decided to ask Edward Adams, the civil servant who was running the supreme court project, to meet her. "He said I am going to introduce you to the guy who is going to lead the project. I went and met him, we had a chat . . . Once I was in, I knew my [résumé] would be okay. There was a point where I had been let in the door, and I knew I could stand alone."

The hiring process was short. By the time her children had gone back to school at the end of the first week of September in 2003, she had started work. It's hard to join a government bureaucracy. Lauren began with a contract "almost as precarious as a consultancy," said McDonald, who pointed out that this way he was able to recruit her without running an internal competition.

The supreme court project took about a year. Lauren's group was responsible for creating a policy and then drafting legislation that they saw all the way through the House of Commons and the Lords. Lauren wrote the formal submissions, which McDonald described as "works of art."

She loved the work. She fit in well with her team, and Keith remembered, "She was meeting and working with very smart, nice people. And it was good to see her reengaged by the issues and stimulated by the people she worked with."

At the end of that year, England had an embryonic new supreme court and Lauren had a London entry on her résumé. Her success on that project led to another attractive offer from Andrew McDonald: a review of Britain's human rights division in a post-9/11 world. This was an area where her experiences in South Africa had some resonance. With the Home Office pushing through tough new counter-terrorism laws, which mirrored similar legal changes in the United States, and with detention without trial becoming a common concept in the free world, Lauren was once again dealing with the rights of the individual.

If the Home Office represented the government, then her department, the DCA, was there to represent its citizens. She wrote a plan for restructuring (or as she put it, "greatly expanding") the human rights division. Her aim was to increase her department's presence, and she was successful. "My entire presentation was implemented," she said with pride.

For both of those projects she had worked on a contract. When she accepted the next governmental offer, she became a staff policy adviser. This time she was working on the newly introduced Freedom of Information Act. This department had a heavy workload. For the first time in England both ordinary people and journalists were able to request what had once been protected information. Governmental departments were inundated with disclosure requests, and the new law demanded that those requests be answered within a prescribed time period. The DCA was responsible for making sure the system worked. It was also the clearinghouse to which all tricky government requests were sent for assessment.

Like Judith Feder, Lauren was at a different stage in her career than most of her co-workers.

All these very young, ambitious, thrusting twenty-something-year-olds were looking to make their names in the division and were working long evenings and weekends, and it was a fairly "testosteroney" environment, with people outdoing each other in terms of the number of hours they could work, the number of requests they could process, and the number of *tricky* requests they could process. It did make me realize that I was way beyond that point of proving myself while working, and I was on a very different career trajectory from a lot of the people around me. And I guess it started to help me crystalize why I was working.

All working mothers feel a pang at some point when they miss their children. Lauren felt hers every day at four o'clock, when she knew that Sam and Miles were getting out of school. She wanted to be there. It was different when she loved what she was doing. Now that she was working in an environment she didn't find terribly appealing, she began to question why she was bothering at all.

In the middle of all of this her father died. His death was a devastating loss to her. Her eyes still filled with tears when she looked at his photograph two years after his death, and she said she had not once been able to look at his picture without crying.

Then came the London bomb attacks of July 2005—seven years after the Johannesburg mugging. Suddenly Lauren felt overwhelmingly unsafe. Her *children* were no longer safe. She had brought them to a new country to protect them. And for what? With the realization that England was as dangerous a place to be as anywhere else in the world, she broke down and suffered what she described as a "massive panic attack."

The two psychological blows caused Lauren not just to question her professional life, but also to examine how it affected her domestic one. Her London salary didn't make much of a difference at home once she had carved out a chunk for babysitting help. Her office in Whitehall was difficult to get to from Hampstead. The open-plan layout made it uncongenial to children. The environment wasn't fun, and she'd had enough of it. Her experience of working in London had given her the confidence to know that if she took some time off, she would work again. She knew what she didn't like, and she knew what she wanted. She wanted to go home and take care of her boys.

In February 2006, after she had moved one more time to work as part of a team advising on Legal Aid—a job she found dreary—she resigned. She immediately began mulling over a number of entrepreneurial ideas with a variety of friends. She thought about buying investment properties with a Spanish friend or starting a professional networking group for women in England. It never occurred to her that she wouldn't work again, but she was in no rush. At times she talked about staying at home for several years, maybe even until the boys left school. She had the confidence to wait for what felt right when it felt right. "Something's going to come along," she said.

I was already deep into interviewing Lauren at the time of her resignation, and it initially threw me. She had quit her comeback! But the more I heard the confidence in her voice, the more appealing her story (and her attitude) sounded. Why shouldn't she quit? It wasn't as if she was going to be at home forever. There is nothing wrong

with serial comebacks. If you can do it once, you can do it twice—
or more. The job that you come back to might be the perfect way
back in, but it might not be what suits you for the long haul.

Lauren stayed at home for a year, happy because she was there for
her boys and connected to the outside world through a diverse social
life. She had always wanted her work to have some kind of social
meaning, and she found that as she grew older, this concern was becoming even more important. She had always wanted to make a
difference—and in fact she always had. As she settled into middle
age, a new job appeared to synthesize all the elements of her past
and present and take her into the future.

Lauren had always had a strong social conscience, but like many
mothers, now that she had children, she began to think about kids
who were less fortunate than her own. Now the focus to give back
was child-based. She still wanted to be at home with her boys, she
still wanted to control her schedule, she still had the pull of South
Africa. Was there anything she could do that would bring all of
these elements together?

The opportunity presented itself in spring of 2007 through another
friendship, this time with a fellow South African, David Altschuler.
Altschuler was a financier married to a trauma counselor and psy-
chotherapist. The couple had a long history of involvement with
charitable projects. The Colemans became friendly with the
Altschulers and began to support their London charity, the One to
One Children's Fund. One to One had been created to back social
and educational projects all over the world. Its mandate was both to
relieve the poor, the suffering, and the neglected and "to help children overcome the trauma of war, prejudice and natural disaster."

The charity already had a strong presence in South Africa, largely
because of David Altschuler's background. But it had satellite offices
around the world in countries where children needed help. In South
Africa it worked with local hospitals to treat pediatric HIV/AIDS.
It provided trauma counseling in Kosovo, tsunami relief in Kerala,

pediatric equipment to Belarus, and day-care centers and after-school programs to children throughout the Middle East. Its aim was not just to help kids in need but to find a way of bringing together children who would otherwise grow up to live apart. This was an understandable aspiration for a South African. Which was why in the spring of 2007, when David Altschuler called Lauren to ask if she would be interested in taking over One to One as managing director, she was immediately intrigued. But she was older and wiser, so . . . "I said it's too big, but have you thought about job sharing?"

Lauren was all about relationships. So she picked a mother from her book group ("I'm so bloody impulsive") who was looking to do more with her time. But Lauren chose her deliberately, because her background and experience was a good complement to her own.

The friend she picked was an English journalist turned communications consultant, who had worked at Reuters and knew and understood the world of charities. Together the two women researched job sharing for a proposal they presented to One to One's trustees. They would share everything. They'd have one e-mail address, a double-sided business card, three separate days and one overlapping day in the office. They pointed out that the organization would essentially be getting two people for 1.2 times the cost and a complete set of skills and experiences impossible to find in one person.

Lauren designed her dream setup in much the same way she had done when she started her own law firm. One crucial element was already in place—the One to One office was only ten minutes from her house. She could get there by 8:30, put in eight hours of work, and be home in time to get her boys off the school bus. This could be a job that would finally give her "freedom from the tyranny of child care." "Those logistics are incredibly important," she said as she waited to hear when she could start. "I could have been offered the most exciting job in the world, and if it were two hours away on the tube, I'd have said no. I don't want to be an hour and a half away from my children again."

Being close to home and therefore losing the need for child care in turn affected how she saw her salary, which she described as "fine, but not private sector." Working didn't bring its own set of expenses. Her salary could be free money. In early July 2007 Lauren heard that her proposal to job-share had been accepted. Now when she returned to South Africa she could have a connection and a sense of purpose. She could work on her visits there and continue to live in London, where she was happy and relatively safe. And as it turned out, sharing a job would be yet another transition. Six months later, when her friend decided to leave the charity, Lauren happily took over as its sole director.

The week that she began her new job in 2007, two cars filled with explosives were found in London, and an SUV crashed into Glasgow International Airport. The world would always be unsafe. But the extra year at home and the way she had designed her job had made it easier for her to come to terms with this reality. And if she didn't spend her working days making the world a safer place, she would try to make it seem less frightening to thousands of young children.

On the morning of her first day back she sent me an e-mail from home. "Off now with my shiny new shoes and bag to change the world and be back in time for the school run," she wrote. And then she left for work.

Ellen Warner

A woman's best production is a little money of her own.
                                        Clare Boothe Luce

ELLEN WARNER BECAME a photographer thirty-five years ago in New York. "Photographer" is a job description that tells you less than you think. Is Ellen an artist or a journalist? Does she shoot fruit bowls or fashion spreads? Portraits or landscapes? Does she exhibit? Is she able to sell her work? If so, who buys it and in what form? How much money does she make? Has she become rich from her work, or does she make a living? Can she even break even?

Other careers, such as law, teaching, or sales, are relatively easy to explain. Careers in the arts can take many different forms. Annie Leibovitz is a photographer, but she is also Annie Leibovitz, which seems to be its own job title. Ellen Warner is not Annie Leibovitz and doesn't have her career. But over the years she has managed to produce a solid body of work. She now has her own Web site, of course, where she displays a number of her pictures along with a coherent summary of what she's done and what she can do.

A couple of years ago Ellen had an exhibition of her work at a gallery in Soho, New York—her first exhibition in more than ten years. She had started her career as a photojournalist in 1969. She stopped working professionally for ten years when her children were small. This was her comeback moment after years of being a wife and mother and an active volunteer in her community.

When she left photography in 1978 to raise her two daughters, Alix and Lily, she did so wholeheartedly. She was absolutely engrossed in her children. In the early days her identity as their mother sustained her sense of herself. She was so rooted in her household that she never thought to take pictures of it. She barely took pictures on vacation. What had been a consuming career that took her all over the world didn't easily downgrade to a part-time hobby. When people asked her whether she was photographing, she would dismiss them with a "Been there, done that."

Such an absolute departure from her work meant that when she decided to return to it, she had to do so incrementally. When you are in the production business, you have to have something to sell. Ellen had to shoot her way back into her career print by print. Seen that way, the evening of her comeback opening was more of a turning point rather than a beginning. This was the moment she had been working toward for several years—the moment when round two of her career might become lucrative. In a business like photography you invest a lot before you can begin to think of returns.

Perhaps because it had been such a long time coming, the atmosphere on the late fall night of her opening felt especially celebratory. The walls of the small downtown gallery were covered with photographs. There was a total of fifty-eight prints available for sale in limited editions of twenty each. The title of the show was Portraits and Desert Life. The photographs on display were from a number of different countries: England, the United States, Greece, Morocco, and Egypt. One wall was covered with portraits of well-respected authors and people you felt you might know, of different ages and in a variety of poses—seated, standing, in a garden, on a porch, looking away or directly at the camera. The other walls contained images from other worlds: portraits of young women or girls in remote desert oases; men in djellabas playing dominoes; people going about their days in dusty market squares, leading their sheep and cattle through streets or across fields; praying, playing games; preparing and eating their food.

The contrast between the still, sunlit, unhurried worlds on display and the bustling, animated gallery on that crisp New York night was striking. But both worlds were part of Ellen's business. The two hundred guests attending the opening night were all potential customers, even the friends and family. There wasn't exactly pressure to buy, but people bought. This gallery opening was its own marketplace, sparkling and gleaming, with canapés and white wine offered alongside pictures that cost from seven hundred dollars for some of the author portraits to twenty-five hundred dollars for the larger desert scenes.

In the middle of it all was the vivacious picture of the photographer greeting her guests. That night Ellen Warner was excited and animated—unusual for a woman whose normally gentle personality is more contemplative than effervescent. She stood in the center of the room, relaxed, socially at ease, and poised—a slim and elegant woman, with well-groomed auburn hair; high cheekbones; and clear, bright, lightly tanned skin. In her long flowing tunic over black pants and a light brown scarf draped just so around her neck, she was a portrait of a graceful, artistic WASP. But if one looked closely, around her neck was a heart-shaped stone, made into a pendant and attached to a necklace of string by one of the Bedoin she'd traveled the desert with.

Ellen's ambition that night was to sell twelve photographs. She ended up selling twenty-two. This was a show the gallery described as doing "extremely well." It sold more than they expected and more than they usually sell at such openings.

Scratch the surface of any art form and you will find a business. To discuss the relative success of Ellen Warner's comeback, we have to define what success means in a field like hers. In Ellen's art—or let's call it business—success is less about salary, benefits, or promotion than freedom and status.

You might agree that it's more prestigious to be the photographer whose picture appears in the *New York Times* than it is to be the editor who commissions the work. But it's the editor who gets paid every week and has health insurance and a 401(k), not the photographer. In fact, the editor can easily make far more per hour than the photographer. The same model is true for all visual artists, and it is true for writers, from freelance journalists like me to poets, screenwriters, and authors of fiction. We live hand-to-mouth and—when they come in—we often spend our checks in their entirety, forgetting we'll have tax bills to pay down the line. Like our friends in the music and theater businesses—the composers, dancers, and musicians—the product we are selling is our own ability. But we cannot work alone. In order to make a living we need to have a filter of other professionals—agents, managers, editors, gallery owners, or producers—who are subsidized by the money we make.

Ellen, like most photographers, is also expected to subsidize her own work. This is regarded as the investment part of her business. Most of the time her investment includes the obvious—buying her own expensive cameras, paying for her own film, paying to have that film developed or developing it herself (most photographers send it out these days). She also has to pay for a high-quality printer and cartridges. She needs a studio to work in and storage space for her equipment and prints. And even when she is on commission, she might have to cover her own travel expenses, though if she's working for a publication like the *New York Times Magazine*, she'll get paid expenses, a day rate, and a page rate for what is essentially a one-time use of a picture.

Often she has to wait for her paycheck, even when she is working on commission. Reimbursement for expenses doesn't come quickly, either. While she is waiting she has to find the money to pay all of her bills, including those she incurred while working on behalf of the commissioning organization. Photographers live and work on credit cards, so they need to sustain good credit. In order to sustain good credit they need to pay their bills. Which takes money . . .

It's true that there are photojournalists on staff at news organizations who don't live hand to mouth (although their numbers are on the decline). Working beats and shifts, they cover presidents and parades, wars and sports alongside their print companions for salaries, benefits, and two or three weeks of vacation a year, just as if they had "normal" jobs. Their lives are different from the portrait photographer who works on commission. A successful portrait photographer is someone like Tina Barney, who photographs her subjects in a kind of highly stylized pseudo-snapshot format and sells her work for thousands of dollars. These days it might be bought by families, but it's also snapped up by collectors and housed in the Museum of Modern Art in New York. Barney recently shot an ad campaign for Theory, and she produces books with a list price of fifty dollars. But she is an anomaly.

Fortunately for Ellen, the last few years have seen an explosion in the photography market. More private collectors are focusing on photography as art than ever. In 2006 the *New York Times* noted, "An increasing number of collectors to the photography market . . . have in turn driven the market to new heights . . . Whether it is the romance of the photographic image or the allure of a choice investment that attracts a collector, new rules and newcomers alike have changed the photography landscape."

If photography is the new art, would that make Ellen Warner an artist? Would we change our definition of her success if we thought of what she did differently? The photographer Henri Cartier-Bresson described photography as "a craft. Many want to turn it into an art form, but we are simple craftsmen who must do their work well." Ellen defines success as something that is measured in terms of "if you feel you've achieved what you set out to achieve."

"Your own feeling is the bottom line," she told me when I asked her to give me a sense of what is considered successful in her world. I kept coming back to this thought as I considered her career. There is no doubt that she has been successful. She has made money, and she is doing what she loves. But her story seems to have more of a struggle about it than any of the others, which is ironic when you learn she comes from perhaps the most privileged background of all.

Like Tina Barney, Ellen Warner began her photographic career taking family portraits. Her decision to make photography her career was straightforward. You can imagine people everywhere having the same idea. She went on vacations, took pictures, and liked it. In her case, the pleasure she got from photography happened at exactly the right time—on a college graduation trip around America. Just when she was meant to be deciding what she wanted to do with her life, she realized she loved seeing the world through a lens.

But the world Ellen came from wasn't one where women were expected to pursue careers. This was a world where the female family members worked hard—but not for money. Ellen's female relatives volunteered. They offered their services to art museums, churches, schools, and soup kitchens. They were the wives and daughters of the well-heeled, Republican members from the northeastern banking and legal establishments. They were quintessential WASPs, with the no-nonsense sense of service and duty that came with their enjoyment of privilege. You wouldn't have found a woman from this background running a bank or chairing a law firm. Her way of earning a little extra would have been much more genteel. But photography as a way of life formed the perfect bridge between the traditions of Ellen's background and the modern world in which she came of age.

In her book *A History of Women Photographers*,[1] Naomi Rosenblum noted that women have been actively involved with photography "ever since the medium was first introduced in 1839." They were drawn to it professionally and personally, she pointed out, "finding it an effective means both to earn a living and to express ideas and feelings."

The Yankee women of Ellen's family didn't really have to earn a living or express their feelings. They were well-educated activists in their own small corner of the world. It was an unusual family in that its women members were given exactly the same educational opportunities as the men. They had their minds opened, yet their professional opportunities remained closed. Their path through life was laid out before them, and they were expected to walk through it unquestioningly. Indeed the men followed their own paths, too, into Wall Street, working for law firms or banks. This was tradition, and it was equally binding for both men and women.

Ellen didn't fit the pattern at all. For a start, she did not go to Harvard. The family wasn't just well educated, it was *Harvard* educated, and Ellen didn't get in. She told me she hadn't gone to Harvard shortly after I met her. Her mother told me so, too—shortly after I met *her*. In fact, everyone in her family told me at some point or another that Ellen Didn't Go to Harvard. Unlike her grandfather (acting dean of Harvard Law), her mother (Radcliffe, then Barnard after her marriage), her father (Harvard), her brothers (Harvard) and sisters (Radcliffe), and her husband (Harvard), Ellen didn't make it.

Everything in her adult life seems to have been defined by this failure of acceptance. But Ellen had a drive that easily matches—you might even say surpassed—those members of her family who went and graduated from Cambridge. It is that rejection, she told me, that gave her ambition.

She was born Ellen Murphy, the daughter of Grayson and Mary. Grayson was the senior hardworking partner of a large New York law firm. His wife ruled over her family with a firm hand and a sharp tongue. Weekends and summers were spent out of the city—up and down the East Coast for shorter periods of time, Europe for longer breaks. Children had nannies and went to private school. Sunday mornings took place in church. Mealtimes and bedtimes were on a strict schedule. Parents were affectionate but distant. Standards were high.

Mary Murphy, Ellen's mother, was an exceptionally bright woman who had graduated from high school at sixteen and headed off to Radcliffe as expected. Mary's father, Joseph Warren, had spent more than thirty years teaching property law at Harvard Law School, rising to become acting dean before retiring. He committed suicide in 1942 after a long struggle with depression. In an issue of *Harvard Law Review* dedicated to him after his death, he was described as a man of few words, a kind man who possessed a "puritanical integrity that sometimes was almost stubborn in its tenacity." "Gentleman Joe" was known by all on campus as standing "for all that has made the true New England gentleman honored wherever he is known."[2]

The Warren family members were doctors as well as lawyers. Here again they were at the top of their field. Not just the top, but the forefront. Dr. John Warren, a surgeon during the American Revolution, had been a founding member of Harvard Medical School. His son, John Collins Warren, was a founder of the *New England Journal of Medicine* (still famous for being the first surgeon to operate using anesthesia). Four generations down from the original John Warren, his great-great grandson, who was also named John Warren, also studied medicine at Harvard. He veered off from surgery to teach anatomy. His nephew, Richard, Mary's brother, returned to the fold and became Harvard Medical School's Professor of Surgery. Today there is a Warren Building at Massachusetts General Hospital and a Warren Museum at Harvard Medical School.

Obviously Mary Warren was never going to become a doctor—or even a lawyer. Though she had been well educated (as was her own mother, Constance—a member of the first graduating class from Bryn Mawr in 1901), she kept to the family tradition by not becoming a professional woman but instead the wife of a professional man. At the age of twenty, Mary married a lawyer, Grayson Mallet-Prevost Murphy, and began her career as a wife. Seventy years later I asked her if she had ever been interested in law herself. "Not at all," she replied. "Although I would much rather sit next to a lawyer than a businessman at dinner."

By the time Ellen was born in 1948, the family household was well established in a townhouse on East Sixty-second Street in Manhattan. Her father, the son of an investment banker, was working his way up through the ranks as a lawyer, and would eventually become senior partner at Shearman and Sterling in New York.

Mary was thirty-five years old when Ellen was born, and already had three children—a boy and two girls. After Ellen she would have one more son. She was a difficult mother, simultaneously devoted to her children and yet their fiercest critic. She would do anything for them and loved them intensely but was never comfortable actually *being* with them. Tall, with a military bearing and strong blue eyes, her physical presence was intimidating. Her expression was mainly forbidding, but when she smiled, her whole face softened and became quite lovely. What her children feared the most, though, was her tongue, which was acerbic and could be lacerating. She was disparaging, demanding, and scornful of any emotional outpouring. "She made all her children feel insecure and shy," said Ellen.

Mary ran a household that was filled with routine, where emotions were kept in check, though tempers were often lost. "My only strength is organization," she said to me when I went to visit her in her Fifth Avenue apartment. She spoke with deliberate self-deprecation, sitting surrounded by pictures of her grandchildren. She had become softer over time. But not much. She couldn't understand why I would be interested in her daughter's career; it was a subject that she herself didn't find remotely interesting. Her own interests as a younger woman had been in the arts. She was passionate about music. She loved to sing and sang ("very badly") with a choral society. She also loved gardening and Ellen got her love of travel from her mother. Later in life Mary became a member of the board of the New York Botanical Garden and often went with a group of fellow enthusiasts to hunt for flowers in the Pyrenees or the Dolomites.

Her coldness might have come from the same depression her father suffered from, but if it did she wasn't aware of it. She never felt depressed, she said, though she confessed to a lingering feeling of hopelessness as a younger woman. She said she used to wonder why she was getting up in the morning. But, she added, she would feel better having had something to eat.

Like many children of her background, Ellen's emotional warmth came from her nanny. Unlike her older sisters and brother, who had grown up under the disciplinary hand of a German nanny, Ellen had an Irish "Nana." Nana was the polar opposite of her employer. She wore a fur coat in a family of cloth. She was a Catholic, who went regularly to church to light candles, taking her young charge with her. On her days off she'd go to the theater. She was cozy, warm, and full of life. She had a large network of nanny friends who took care of a variety of children from privileged backgrounds. Through Nana, Ellen became best friends at the age of four with Lindsay Crouse, the daughter of the musical playwright Russel Crouse. And she went to a birthday party at the Stork Club at five.

Ellen saw her mother at teatime. Mary had her breakfast sent up on a tray while the children ate in the dining room with their father. They had the same breakfast every day of their lives—poached egg on toast with bacon and a piece of toast on the side. On Sundays kidneys would be added. The tradition was so unchanging that when Ellen went for her first sleepover at the age of seven and was offered scrambled eggs for breakfast, she was shocked. "It was like another country!"

The distance the children may have felt from their mother was offset for Ellen by the presence of her father. Ellen felt very close to him. They had a special bond. "He used to say to me, 'You were my first postwar child.' And I would ask, 'Was that good?' and he would say it was good—it was very, very good."

Dinnertimes included the whole family, and Ellen found them formal and dull, with a lot of talk about history and her mother expressing frustration at her father's reticence. He was a man of few words, who in those days didn't seem to be the companion his wife craved. But at breakfast he delighted his children with stories of the good witch Beatrice, and the giant Rollo, and the bad witch Clara. After breakfast he would go around the table kissing each child on the top of their head before walking them to the bus stop. "He was very cozy. I would sit on his lap. I always felt that he thought I was pretty and enchanting. I never knew whether or not he thought that I was bright. The frivolous one—that was my role."

When they were young, the Murphy children spent weekends in the city going to church with their father while their mother stayed at home. Religion was never discussed in the household. "We just went." As for school, that had its tradition, too. Like her sisters, Ellen was destined for the Chapin School, although academically she felt inadequate from early on. This was partly because—like her mother—she was young for her year. Like her sisters, she went from Chapin to Miss Porter's boarding school. "The first day of class I was late for Latin, because I had got lost somewhere in the school, and when I arrived, the Latin teacher said, 'I'm so glad you're here; your sister was the brightest girl I had in my class.' I then got a D."

Ellen graduated from Miss Porter's when she had just turned eighteen. Her sisters and her older brother had all been A students, working hard throughout school and often getting up at 5:30 in the morning to study. As she had followed them from school to school, it was expected that Ellen would follow them on to college, but she hadn't been so driven. "I was the first person in my family not to go to Harvard since the year dot. My mother was furious at Harvard that I didn't get in, and I remember her saying, 'I will never give them another penny,' but I shouldn't have got in. I was a B student." Ellen certainly felt that her mother was upset, but worse than that, "I felt stupid."

After her rejection by Harvard, Ellen enrolled at Wheaton College in Norton, Massachusetts ("not a major university," commented her mother when she described it to me). She chose it because it was physically close to Cambridge, but that was as far as the tradition pulled. Her college years liberated her from many of the imposed standards of her childhood. Finally, she began to enjoy her education. She chose art history as her major, a subject that gave her "pure enjoyment." Living in a co-ed environment away from home for the first time also made her aware that she was attractive to men. She had always been a good-looking girl. "The beauty in the family" was how her older sister Patty described her. She was the only one of the five children to have her portrait painted as a child.

Traditionally the Warren and the Murphy women married either during their college years or shortly after graduation. Ellen's sister Patty, who had been accepted by both Bryn Mawr and Radcliffe (the "weight of tradition" decided where she went, she said) had studied art history, too. She had taught for a year before marrying her brother's best friend. "I had known him my whole life." Ellen's second sister never worked before her marriage to a banker.

But times were changing. Being born after the war made a difference. The motto of the headmistress of the Chapin School in the 1950s was "Be conspicuous by being inconspicuous." The motto of her successor in the 1960s and 1970s changed to "Stand up and be counted for."

Immediately upon graduating from college in 1969, Ellen took one thousand dollars she inherited from a great-aunt and left town on a road trip. With some friends she drove down through Richmond, Virginia, then on to Nashville, Tennessee, before crossing Mississippi, and ending up in Mexico. "It was freedom."

It was also light-years away from her childhood. Traveling around America in the 1960s as a young adult introduced her to the world in a way that none of her European trips as a child had. "It was just all new," Ellen remembered. "The Grand Ole Opry, Natchez, the feeling of history, then the wide-open spaces, the skies of Texas, the desert of northern Mexico, the relaxed humor of it all . . . watching the first man land on the moon with "Mack the Knife" playing in the background, the Austrian boyfriend who bought me thirty-six roses, the mariachi serenading us, sleeping on the beach under San Simeon, the usual stuff of innocent girls discovering a world . . . feeling pretty and free, no more work of college; life was ahead."

She took a Konica camera with her and spent the trip taking pictures like any other tourist. After her trip ended in California, she returned to New York and a respectable job editing grant applications for the Ford Foundation. But she decided she wanted to pursue photography, so her second year she negotiated a deal with the Ford Foundation to work only in the mornings so she could enroll at the Germain School of Photography, located in the basement of the transportation building on lower Broadway in New York in the afternoons. This was to be a technical rather than artistic training. The yearlong professional career course gave her a decent grounding in photographing fashion, architecture, and portraiture. "Mostly stuff I never used again." She graduated from the Germain School in 1971 and immediately started work as a freelance photographer.

Both Ellen's reputation and her confidence got a boost when she won one of five places to take photographs of New York City for a permanent display at the Statue of Liberty. The assignment lasted for six months and was supervised by Tom Orr, then photo editor of *Newsweek*. Day and night, by foot or on ferry, from high in a helicopter or underground in the subway, from borough to borough, she and her fellow photographers shot color pictures capturing the essence of New York City. The photos were exhibited at the Statue of Liberty until its restoration in the 1980s.

From the start, she combined photojournalism with portraiture. Taking portraits gave her a frisson as she connected with her subjects. Photography didn't impede her social life. Through an old boyfriend she met a young lawyer named Miner Warner. After they met, Ellen started running into him all over the place, but he never asked her out. So she took the initiative and decided to ask him to her family's Christmas party. "I told my father I had met someone called Miner Warner and he said, 'I know Miner Warner,' and it turned out he worked at my father's law firm."

In many ways Miner was perfect for Ellen. He was brilliant. In fact, he had attended Harvard! He also came from impressive WASP lineage; his ancestor didn't just arrive on the Mayflower, he was also its captain. Miner was a lawyer who would shortly move over to investment banking. He loved to read and to travel. He had been taking trips abroad alone since he was sixteen years old. After earning his degree from Harvard, he had studied at the London School of Economics and at Sciences Po in Paris.

Miner Warner was a complicated man. He combined a sweet gentleness with a brusque, competitive exterior. He had an idealistic, almost romantic view of his place in the world, but he was not a romantic boyfriend, and Ellen wouldn't find him to be a romantic husband. He neglected to make a toast to her at their wedding, which he mentioned when I talked to him. Yet he added that he was as nervous as he had ever been the week before their marriage. He never gave Christmas or birthday presents, nor flowers on Valentine's Day. He was insecure yet kind; he could be socially awkward, but he loved socializing. His politics were right-wing, and he was a devout Episcopalian. He strongly believed in his duty to serve his community and did so. He was a clubman who went often and enthusiastically to the Brook and Links clubs. Yet the clubby, albeit competitive, atmosphere of Wall Street banks and brokerage firms made him uncomfortable, and he never thrived in that environment.

I asked Ellen what made her want to marry Miner, who seemed so different from the other boyfriends she had had before him. She pointed out that at the time of meeting him she had moved back home and that her father really liked him. Then she gave me a checklist of four things he had going for him.

1. There was the intellectual thing that was so appealing to me.
2. He was what I was not.
3. He was an escape route.
4. He was a very kind and tenderhearted person. I knew he wouldn't hurt me. I knew he could be counted upon.

Finally, she added that by marrying Miner she was giving her family something she thought they wanted—a well-educated intellectual companion. With Miner installed as the academic credentials, Ellen could be free to be creative.

Miner and Ellen were married in 1972. They spent their honeymoon in India, where Ellen took pictures to send back to the States and Miner carried her tripod all over the place for her. "And I never used it, just photographed without it."

The following year Ellen was included in a *New York Magazine* article about portrait photographers. She was described as "a talented newcomer to the field who takes beautiful pictures at affordable prices: what is more she has a gentleness that puts children at ease." The article said that she charged $38.50 for a black-and-white sitting that would take an hour and a half and include three eight-by-ten prints. If she photographed a family for a day, she charged $95.00 plus travel expenses. Her prices were more than affordable. By the standards of the other photographers mentioned in the piece, they were ridiculously cheap. She was charging less than 25 percent of some of the others, who sounded no less qualified or experienced than she was.

Why did she charge so little? It was a deliberate strategy. "I wanted to get into the market, and I was no one compared to some of the others in the article. I agree it was nothing, but one has to remember thirty-six dollars, or whatever it was, was *something* in those days, and I got *lots* of business from the article."

As she built up her reputation, she saw her work as a straightforward business enterprise, where the aesthetics lay in the good looks of her well-groomed subjects and the attractive surroundings they sat in. It was possible to make a lot of money doing this kind of work. Did she see it as a career? She did.

In his book *Aging Well* George E. Vaillant, MD, director of the Harvard Study of Adult Development, sets out four criteria that transform a job or hobby into a career. They are contentment, compensation, competence, and commitment.[3] Ellen possessed all four of the criteria, but she always had to combine her career with life with her husband, and she had to contend with a family that never really saw what she was doing as more than a hobby.

In the early days of their marriage the Warners traveled extensively together to India, Ceylon, China and Southeast Asia, Turkey, and Iran. Ellen would organize the trips so that she could take pictures, some preassigned, some on spec, but who in her world considered it work? Did anyone, including her husband, take what she was doing seriously? Her sister Patty explained the family's attitude. "Work in the arts was a hobby—taking pictures with our little Brownie cameras on holiday. We didn't understand it as a career possibility, because we hadn't grown up with it. Careers were something you worked at in an office five days a week." Ellen's husband confessed that to him, too, it was "more than a hobby, less than a calling."

In 1974 the Warners moved to England. Miner had been sent by the investment bank Salomon Brothers to London to help expand its offices there. Now his work sent him all over the world. He went from Europe to the Middle East to Latin America and Asia. He was seldom home. Even when he was in London he worked long hours, staying in the office as markets opened in other parts of the world.

Ellen didn't sit at home waiting for him. She had been taken on by the photo agency Black Star, the self-described "primary incubator for the world's best photojournalists." Black Star sold her photographs to magazines and newspapers around the world. Now if she accompanied Miner on his trips, she would have her own itinerary and would send pictures back.

She went with him to Iran and Turkey in 1973. In Iran she had her own guide provided by the government. "I'm sure he was assigned to keep an eye on me—so I wandered everywhere with him, the guide, not Miner." After that there was one big trip a year, either with Miner or on her own. China in 1974, Kenya in 1975, Japan in 1976. It was easy for her to make friends in England, and new friends led to more work. She started photographing families in London as she had done in New York. But now she broadened her range and took every assignment that came her way. She would photograph performing arts groups, educational institutions, even politicians. On one occasion she was sent to photograph Margaret Thatcher, who had just been elected leader of the Conservative Party in England.

In 1978 Alix Warner was born in London. Ellen was twenty-nine. Her photographic assignments had dwindled the year before Alix's birth. She had enjoyed being pregnant and had found her drive to work diminished the further along her pregnancy progressed. She also found that her growing success had made Miner less rather than more supportive of her work. In his world—as in hers—wives and mothers didn't work for a living. His desire for her to be at home made it hard for her to go out and photograph the world. Becoming a mother resolved the conflict that had arisen in the marriage over Ellen's work. "There was no adjustment," she said. "I loved having [Alix]. It was like stepping off the world into a part of eternity. I loved being a mother. I didn't miss photography at all."

When Alix was a few months old the Warners moved back to New York and bought a small townhouse on the Upper East Side one street away from Ellen's sister Patty. Ellen had returned to live the same life she had been brought up in. But she was never quite as traditional as she was meant to be. Instead of an Irish nanny, she hired Yo-Yo Ma's mother to take care of Alix. "I found her through a friend who was married to a Chinese man," she explained.

She was the best. She loved to be outdoors and kept saying to Alix, "Let's exercise." They would endlessly lie on the floor legs in the air, "exercising." She was a superb cook—she bought us a steamer and would drink the water left at the bottom after cooking vegetables—to get the vitamins. She constantly complained about Yo-Yo—"What a mess he is! Always throws his towels on the floor, and leaves them there." Once I heard Yo-Yo on TV saying that Chinese parents do not cuddle, they instruct—and I remember that whenever Alix fell down and came running to Mrs. Ma for comfort, Mrs. M. would pat her and say, "Next time be more careful."

Technically, Ellen could now be described as a stay-at-home mother, but the women of her family didn't stay at home with their children all day. Her sister Patty, who had found the early years of her three children's lives overwhelming, was beginning to volunteer at a center for parents and children. She hoped to pass on some wisdom from her own experience. By the time I met her in 2006 she had been educating parents and children for twenty-six years—and had no desire to stop.

Ellen didn't begin to volunteer seriously until after the birth of her second daughter, Lily. It had been a difficult pregnancy and Ellen had been confined to bed for several months. Miner was now working long hours and took his trips by himself. Once again in this book we have the model of a father who spends long stretches of time away from home, leaving his wife alone as a single parent. Note that the travel occurs during her nonworking period. Ellen, like Judith and Lauren, didn't feel that her time at home with her children was a sacrifice. Yet, as in those cases, it wasn't just possible because of her husband's career—it was necessary.

"He really wasn't around much when we were growing up," remembered Alix about her father. "He traveled a lot, constantly with work. He would come home really just exhausted from work and not want to talk with the family but want to unwind and be with a book," said Alix. "I think he was much more the absent parent, underfunctioning if you will. Because of that my mother was overfunctioning and would sometimes be controlling and overbearing, but I think it was because she was picking up the role of both parents in many ways."

Residing in the background, just a few blocks away was the girls' maternal grandmother, who hadn't become any more nurturing with age. "When I was little I was totally terrified of her," said Alix. "When I was young and if you cried, she was like, 'If you don't stop crying, I'll give you something to cry for.'"

On his return to New York Miner moved from Salomon Brothers to Merrill Lynch, where he concentrated on domestic and international government loans. The Warners lived an affluent life but not one of excess. Schools were still private, trips were still taken, but this was not a family with an enormous amount of ready cash. In order to live as they did, they had to be careful with both Miner's salary and their investments. This could sometimes lead to strain.

Miner felt enormously driven to make enough money to support his family's lifestyle. But he felt strongly that Ellen should not contribute to the family paycheck. Any work she did should be of the unpaid kind. Ellen didn't yet feel the need to return to photography, so when the girls were at elementary school, she began volunteering at her church. The Warners worshipped at the Episcopal Church of the Heavenly Rest, a grand gothic structure on the corner of Fifth Avenue and Ninetieth Street. Church members here were affluent, and the church had an endowment of several million dollars.

The church also ran a soup kitchen and gave financial aid to other soup kitchens and community projects around the city. One of these was the Yorkville Common Pantry on 109th Street and Fifth Avenue. This was the part of the city that borders Mount Sinai Hospital, where the Upper East Side flows into Harlem. Founded in 1981 by a coalition of East Side churches and synagogues, the pantry served (and still serves) as both a soup kitchen and a distributor of food around the city. On site there were showers and laundry facilities for the homeless. Those in need were able to receive psychiatric assessments, emergency shelter, and help in obtaining jobs and housing.

This is where Ellen started to spend her time. Like the other mothers in this book, her years at home had sapped her self-confidence. She felt inadequate out in the "real" world. "The volunteer stuff did an enormous amount for me. I realized I was good at organizing people. That I could run things. It made me feel equal to other people. Being an equal in a man's world." She ended up as chair of the board of the Yorkville Common Pantry and senior warden of the Church of the Heavenly Rest. "That's what gave me confidence."

As they got older, the Warners' interests remained similar ("the last of the traditionals," was how Lily described them), but they began to lead more independent lives. They both continued to travel, but their styles were so different that they began to go alone or with the children. Miner was a self-confessed obsessive tourist, who would sightsee in a compulsive way, getting up at the crack of dawn and going to bed at midnight. As he put it, he didn't care what he ate; he cared what he saw. Ellen's style was slightly more languid. She liked sightseeing, but she also liked comfort. To their children it seemed as if they swapped styles when abroad. At home, Alix found her father to be more "laid back," while Ellen was the more "uptight" of the two. In fact, Alix's description of her mother was reminiscent of Ellen's of her own mother.

My mother was always the one my friends were frightened of. Because you could always tell if she didn't like you—I mean with people my age; I am sure it is different among her peers. I think they still remain a little frightened of her, because she has a very competent kind of air. Certainly my mother was always the one to be counted on if there was ever any problem. I mean God bless Dad, but he is not the first person you call if something goes wrong.

Lily, who was interested in art from a young age, found her mother to be a "completely encouraging" maternal figure. Ellen was a constant source of "courage and confidence," strict yet understanding.

The 1990s weren't particularly easy for the family. By 1992 Miner felt Merrill Lynch was squeezing him out, and he left the firm to set up his own financial services company, specializing in international debt restructuring. Working for himself meant he no longer had a regular salary. The family had investment income, but not enough to be a sole source of support. Miner now had the pressure of essentially being a freelancer. And as is often the case, one pressure followed another. In 1995, at the age of fifty-three, he was diagnosed with lymphoma. He was hospitalized and went through chemotherapy. He began to have heart problems and was forced to give up playing tennis—an activity he had loved. His doctors told him to slow down, but he *had* to work. They needed the money. His travel schedule remained intense. When I met him in 2006, he told me he was no longer allowed to walk up stairs, but he had been to Europe three times in the previous six weeks.

The onset of Miner's problems coincided with the girls' adolescence, often a particularly challenging period for New York City parents. Life within the household was stressful, and Ellen needed more of a distraction outside. She also needed to make some money of her own. She had begun taking family portraits again on an ad hoc basis. Now she wanted to expand back into the business and branch out. She wanted to come back and move forward. She saw a niche in photographing authors and began calling literary agents and asking to show them her work. As a way of getting hired, she said she would photograph on spec. If the subjects didn't like her work, she wouldn't get paid. Like the low rates she advertised in *New York Magazine*, it was an investment on her part. "My first author portraits were people done on spec—Marie Brenner, which was used in *Vanity Fair*, and Dominick Dunne's, which was used on the book jacket for *Season in Purgatory* . . . he was the first famous author I photographed. *Vanity Fair* and the publisher, Crown, paid me."

Ellen met the London literary agent Pat Kavanagh through another agent Peter Matson, who was a friend. Kavanagh steered her to the authors Julian Barnes (Kavanagh's husband), Joanna Trollope, and the late Auberon Waugh. Ellen also contacted authors directly herself, picking people who were already well known as she tried to rebuild her portfolio. Her social confidence easily became professional confidence as she made the calls. Over the next several years she photographed Pat Barker, Margaret Drabble, Penelope Fitzgerald, James Fox, Penelope Lively, John Mortimer, Anna Quindlen, and Tom Wolfe—to name a few.

Her work took her regularly to England and away from the pressures of home. This was met with a mixed reception from her husband. "I have to say Ellen didn't receive huge amounts of support from me in terms of her photography," he admitted. "I was preoccupied with my own affairs. And in the mid-nineties it meant she was spending huge amounts of time away when I had lots of stresses. I wasn't dismissive, but I wasn't as supportive as I would have liked to have been. I had a different model; my parents were husband and wife together all the time."

I admired Miner's honesty. It can be hard for a husband who is used to seeing his wife in a set role—often similar to that played by his own mother—to have to adjust his view of her as she breaks out of the traditional mold. Even if a woman was a globe-trotting risk taker in the early days of her marriage, five or ten years as a full-time wife and mother can be comfortable for a man to live with. It's a tough adjustment for a husband to be supportive as his domestic circumstances change. Which is not to say he shouldn't try. Miner's attitude about Ellen's work was picked up by the girls. "I don't think she had too much support from any of us," said Lily, who added that she felt guilty about being unsupportive to her mother when her mother had been so encouraging about her own artistic career.

At lunch with a friend one day Ellen was asked, "Why don't you get back into journalism?" and immediately she felt a a light come back on. Within weeks she had left home for Egypt. Alix was already at college (Kenyon not Harvard), and even though Lily was living at home and going to high school Ellen felt able to leave town. The benefits of her going easily outweighed the disadvantages. She had reached the stage of her life where she wanted to put herself first. "When I am out there doing my thing, I am a different person from the one I am at home. It's hard to articulate, but it's very liberating. I feel like I am an extension of that person I was before marriage . . . The leaving home was always so difficult, but the arriving was always so exciting. When I left I was in a panic, but when I landed I felt a great sense of release and excitement."

Ellen's social confidence and connections gave her an advantage in planning the trip. Friends from the Agency for International Development in Cairo put her in touch with a driver who took people on desert safaris. The car would cost two hundred dollars a day, including the guide, and she and a friend who went with her would pay extra for gas and food.

Her photographs and essay from Egypt, "Sand, Silence and Solitude," was published in the *New York Times* the following year. She was pleased with what she shot, but the next several trips resulted in pictures that seemed to be taken by someone who was increasingly at ease behind the camera. Over the next few years, Ellen continued to take trips, each lasting several weeks, that were elaborate and complicated to set up. Every trip resulted in a published article— sometimes more than one. After Egypt she went to Cuba, which resulted in a piece in *Traveller*. The next year she was in Mongolia for the *New York Times* travel section, then up in Peru's Andes Mountains for *Travel & Leisure* and again the *New York Times*. Personally, she felt herself blossom on these trips. She found that when she connected with people in indigenous cultures in remote parts of the world, she felt more at home than she did in the WASP environment she grew up in.

The Mongolian trip led to her first group show in over twenty-five years. Her pictures were included in a Festival of Mongolia exhibition in the World Financial Center. The more she photographed, the more ambitious she became. She began to think about books, other shows, agents. She found the business of photography—getting her name back out there, getting assignments—time-consuming, hard work. But she was good at it. She had always been a gregarious socializer, good at putting people together, and making the introductions. Now as she put this skill to her own use, it made an interesting contrast. On the one hand she had to be a sophisticated, cosmopolitan extrovert, planning and selling her work. But on assignment she needed to settle into the role of a quiet, careful observer, drawn to indigenous cultures, recording disappearing ways of life.

Financially, she was able to make the photography pay for itself. However, she could only do this by being extremely careful. Her work was not making her rich. She would fly to countries using her frequent flyer miles and try to stay with friends or relatives while away. But she never stinted on her equipment or processing. She shot with a Nikon, a Leica, or a Hasselblad. Some of the cameras she used cost as much as a new car. The lenses were cheaper—about the price of a secondhand car. Family portraits continued to be her most lucrative form of income, so she kept those up, now charging $1,200 for a shoot with two free prints. The author pictures, while interesting and prestigious, didn't pay a fortune—$650 to $700 for a one-time use, $3,000 for world rights. An article with photographs in the travel section of the *New York Times* also paid about $3,000.

In 2004 Ellen's work was included in four group shows in New York, one of which was the Atlantic Gallery. The Atlantic was a co-op gallery owned and run by a group of artists. In order to become a

member, an artist had to submit examples of work and an artist's
statement. The advantage of showing in such a gallery is not just
financial, although co-ops generally take only 10 percent of sales,
compared to the 50 percent of regular galleries. "At a co-op no one is
telling you what to show," Ellen explained. "You can show work that
is interesting but not commercial as well as work that is marketable."

Ellen joined the gallery and immediately started planning her
solo show—her real comeback. She was advised to focus on either
her portraits or her journalism, but she didn't want to choose—she
wanted to represent the full range of her work. Why close any doors
at this point? So she decided to include a little of everything she'd
done over the past several years and hung fifty-five pictures in all.

Hanging fifty-five pictures is an expensive prospect. The show
cost fifty thousand dollars to mount, with Ellen paying for printing,
framing, catalogs, invitations, a public relations mailing, and food
and drink on the night of the opening. She did none of her own developing and printing but worked with Jim Megargee from MV
Labs in New York. She experimented and played around with
everything from contrast to paper texture until she got what she
wanted. The cost to her for each of these prints was seven hundred
dollars. The price to her customers would be twenty-five hundred dollars. Only with that kind of markup did she manage to cover all the
additional costs and just about break even.

Ellen's story didn't end the night her show opened. Of course she
didn't stay frozen, surrounded by her friends and family (except for
her ninety-two-year-old mother, who, ironically, had a heart attack
that same day and had been rushed to the hospital—she subsequently made a full recovery). Her life went on the next morning,
and she had to decide what to do next.

This was about the time that I met Ellen, and although I was impressed with how much she had accomplished in her past, I worried
for her future. It's all very well to work on spec or break even, but
what about her financial security? There was so much to interfere

with her ability to take pictures as she got older. She had already had not just one but two detached retinas—conditions from which she recovered but which had meant she couldn't function as a photographer. During that two-month period of treatment, she couldn't exercise. Not exercising had its own ramifications for someone who carried all of her own—heavy—equipment and had to stay strong and in shape.

Then there were Miner's health problems to consider. I began to wonder what would happen if Ellen outlived Miner. Collecting statistics on the financial futures of women, I began to view everything through the prism of Ellen's circumstances. The average life expectancy for all of us is soaring. In 1900 there were 120 thousand Americans over the age of eighty-five. Today they are the nation's fastest-growing group, and there are more than 4 million of them. Ellen's mother was still alive at ninety-four. If Ellen lived that long, what would her financial security be? Was she looking at a decline in her lifestyle?

I noticed that I began to ask Ellen about money as if I were her agent—or her mother. Meanwhile, she was working hard and her confidence was impressive. Her show had given her new energy. A few months after it she embarked on a massive new project, possibly her most ambitious to date. She began shooting a collection of women age fifty and up from all over the world for a project she called The Second Half. It was an amazing idea, mainly because it consolidated all of her interests and experience. The pictures were all new, a combination of her photojournalism and portrait taking. Some subjects posed becomingly in affluent surroundings; others were caught off guard as they went about their day. She traveled everywhere, shooting women in Greece, England, France, Italy, Algeria, the United States, and the Caribbean, trying to get as much of a cross-section as she could. To accompany each picture she interviewed each woman in order to construct a mini first-person narrative.

The entire project was shot on spec. She did what she could to keep her costs down. She flew on frequent flyer miles; she shot a few author portraits to cover additional expenses. She always stayed with friends and relatives, hardly ever in a hotel. She mined her extensive network for possible subjects. Her faith in her work grew as she progressed, and her enthusiasm never wavered. Over the months, the pictures grew stronger as she relaxed and found a rhythm.

She began to set herself a timetable for showing the collection. She was booked into the same gallery as before, but this time she was more ambitious. She knew that in order to make real money she would have to have better exposure. She began to think in terms of a magazine spread, or a book deal—even some kind of sponsorship.

So this is another picture to keep of her. Mid project. Excited and energized by what she is doing. Planning her next shoot and her next trip. Subsidizing where she can. As happy as she has ever been. Working as hard as she ever has. She's about to turn sixty—the age where working women traditionally began to think about retiring. Sixty? She doesn't look it. She doesn't act it. She feels she's just hitting her stride. She has a show lined up. She will sell her work. She'll break even or do better. She has a future, having turned the "hobby" she fell in love with as a young woman into a multistaged career.

Peg French

*For what is done or learned by one class of women be-
comes, by virtue of their common womanhood, the property of all women.*

Elizabeth Blackwell, MD

WHAT MAKES A good doctor? Empathy? Patience? Compassion? Gentleness? Understanding? Authority? Flexibility? Sensitivity? Wisdom?
Now what makes a good mother? All of these?

It's widely accepted that mothers make good doctors and good
mothers make great doctors. Who could have a better bedside manner than a mother? But medicine is more difficult to combine with
motherhood than almost any other career. Any woman who wants
to be both a doctor and a mother is going to have some tough moments of choice. In a pinch, which should she put first? Her patients
or her children? Should she even have the choice?

From the time that the first women medical students walked into
the all-male teaching Saturday clinics at Pennsylvania Hospital in
Philadelphia to be met with boos and jeers, many men in the profession have thought, no. Some of the male students at the clinic on
that day even threw stones at their female colleagues, acting out the

aggressive sexism that has historically dogged women doctors. The irony is as mystifying as the truth is obvious. If mothers are naturally suited to the nurturing world of medicine, why has it been so hard for them to break through?

Dr. Margaret French, or Peg as she is known, is an anomaly. She is a practicing doctor, a divorcée, and a woman who interrupted her career to stay at home full-time with her children. There are very few Dr. Frenchs out there. It is almost unheard of for a doctor to do what she has done. The push-me-pull-you dynamic of parenting within the medical profession means there are few mothers who take several years off from these careers and then return. Medicine is a difficult career to leave completely for any length of time. Its advances are so constant and so rapid that your knowledge quickly becomes out of date. For that reason, state licensing boards generally ask for a certain number of hours of continuing education per year, with exams at the end. If you want to combine medicine and motherhood, you are more likely to stay and cut back than leave and come back.

But cut back to what? This is not a profession with regular opening and closing times. The hours can be long. One female pediatrician recently expressed a new thought for her fellow doctors: why not cut back to full-time? "Yes, just full-time. Not twelve to fourteen hours a day, six to seven days a week, month after month. By reorganizing one's group, setting limits, and exploring endeavors outside of medicine, the amorphous career octopus could fit back into a reasonable sized box . . . this is a thirty-year marathon, not a five-year sprint."[1]

In order to become a doctor, you have to complete education and training. In order to become a mother, you have to have children. So the first decision an aspiring woman doctor faces is when she should get pregnant. Training takes a long time: four years of college, four years of medical school, then three to eight years of internship and residency, as the paid on-the-job training is called. If you leave home for college at the age of eighteen, you will be a medical student at least until the end of your twenties, possibly well into your thirties, right up until your fertility starts to dwindle.

Peg French is an attractive pathologist in her late fifties, whose expressive hands move fluidly as she speaks and whose face lights up with an animated intelligence as she describes what she does. She came late to medicine and even later to motherhood. Her application to Dartmouth Medical School was made at a stage in her life when she thought she might as well pursue a long-held professional dream, seeing as she wasn't getting married anytime soon. She was thirty years old. She already had a doctorate in clinical pharmacy and was in a post-doctoral program. Medicine appealed to her, but she had previously shied away from it, knowing that she wanted to have kids. In her mind it was tough to have both.

She wasn't exactly wrong. If you take a look at the history of women in medicine, both in the United States and in Europe, you can see that although women doctors generally made professional strides that roughly paralleled the overall gains made by the feminist movement, life was much tougher for mothers.

In 1849 Elizabeth Blackwell became the first American woman to obtain a medical degree. She and her sister went on to create the first hospital where women could receive clinical training from other women, the New York Infirmary for Women and Children. After that the struggles and successes of women doctors followed a parallel, though slightly steeper and more intense, path to that of other working women.

In 1860 there were about two hundred women physicians in the United States. By the end of the nineteenth century there were seven thousand. This progress meant that in the first half of the twentieth century there were a number of firsts. The first woman admitted to the National Academy of Sciences, the first woman doctor to serve in the military, the first woman on the faculty of Johns Hopkins University, the first woman doctor to win a Nobel prize (she shared it with her husband). As feminism gained steam in the second half of the twentieth century, the numbers of women doctors soared, relatively speaking. In 1970 there were roughly twenty-five thousand American women doctors, making up only 7.6 percent of the physician population. Twenty years later that number had quadrupled, and by 2002 over a quarter of doctors in America were women. But it was only in 1990 (the same year the first woman became U.S. Surgeon General) that the first policy report on maternity leave and child care was adopted by the American Medical Association.

Why has there been this divide between women and mothers in this particular profession? Perhaps it has something to do with the traditional view of a woman's role in medicine. Nurses and nuns were long valued for their dedication to a lifetime of service. They were said to have vocations, some kind of divine calling to the work they did. They had no lives of their own. They didn't need them. They weren't supposed to want it all. This combination of drudgery and secular sainthood was enough. It was a myth that prevailed for a long time. But then women started going to medical school, becoming doctors, wanting children, and complaining about glass ceilings. Articles appeared on the subject, such as "Career Problems of Women Doctors," published in the *British Medical Journal* in 1976.[2] At the heart of the problem, the authors wrote, was "the need for part-time work by the mothers of young children." This article stated unequivocally that doctors with children did not want to quit the profession, but they needed fewer hours once they became mothers. Once their domestic responsibilities declined, they were easily able to ramp their professional lives back up. "Most of the doctors wish to return to full-time or nearly full-time work when family responsibilities are fewer," said the authors, pointing out that this was not an unreasonable balance and suggesting that women physicians who wished to raise families should be realistic about the specialties they choose.

Today this has become the widely accepted solution to the challenge of combining motherhood with medicine. Some medical specialties have the reputation of being family friendly, while others are the opposite. In gynecology, pediatrics, or dermatology, for example, it is possible to fix your hours and be on call infrequently enough not to be overwhelmed. Then there is surgery, a field that is generally recognized as being extremely difficult for all women, not just mothers, not just because a bias still exists against women. Surgery is a physically demanding, exhausting field. Surgeons work longer hours than other doctors, are always on their feet, and when they aren't standing still during an operation, they move fast. "I had to follow each surgeon at a dead run or I would lose her," wrote the anthropologist Joan Casell, who followed a group of women surgeons around in the 1990s.[3]

In 1980 three-quarters of the mothers surveyed by the *British Medical Journal* still said that having children had been a handicap to their careers. Yet the fact that they were now asking for on-site child care showed some progress. This time they mentioned the sexism, or "the reactions of senior doctors (generally men)," to the conflicting loyalties of female doctors with children. Perhaps there could be greater understanding from the "men seniors," the authors gently suggested, pointing out that women overwhelmingly came back into the profession full-time once their children were older and they themselves were more experienced. In the end, doctors who were mothers ended up putting in a respectable number of years over the course of their professional lifetimes. Their part-time years seldom numbered more than ten, and they put in twenty-four full-time years. Their major contribution took place from middle age through the final years before their retirement. By then their children had left home and they had maximum experience. Even if you were only looking at this picture with the cold stare of an economist, you might be able to see the value of a highly skilled, experienced, unencumbered member of staff.

Back in the United States, women in the medical profession who had slowly been catching up with the quality-of-life strides made by their colleagues in other careers suffered a setback in the 1980s and

1990s with the onset of managed care. HMOs, looking at the bottom line, impinged on a key aspect of the job that doctors (and particularly women) had enjoyed. Now time was once again a factor, though the juggling act wasn't between work and home; it all took place in the doctor's office. Doctors were now required to see more patients and for less time. Numerous physician work-life studies from this period found that doctors of both sexes were exhausted and disillusioned by the combination of increased workloads and decreased autonomy.

The irony was that as the number of women doctors had grown, so did the number of patients who specifically asked to see a woman. One of the reasons that women doctors were so attractive to sick people was, unsurprisingly, their compassionate bedside manner. They took time. One report identified patients needing women doctors as being the ones with "such time-consuming psychosocial problems as depression, anxiety, and eating disorders."[4] But to HMOs time was money, so time was cut. As the minutes a doctor could spend with her patients were measured and reduced, female doctors' level of job satisfaction fell and their burnout rate rose—at about one and a half times the rate of their male counterparts.

It was right in the middle of this dismal time of cutbacks and paperwork that Peg French had her first child, Aaron. It was 1987 and she was in the first year of her residency. Was this a good time to have a baby? Possibly not. According to the book *Women in Medicine: Career and Life Management*, "Overall, the first year of residency is probably the worst time for a woman physician to have children," due to the expected level of hours and responsibilities.[5] "I don't think there is a good time [to have a baby]," said Peg. "When is the ideal time in your life? There is no good time. It's six of one and half a dozen of the other. When do you have your babies? You have your babies when you finally come up for air and you feel like you can."

Sometimes all the planning in the world doesn't give you the life you want to lead. Peg French was already a late arrival to medicine, and at thirty-seven she was equally late to motherhood. She had planned as best she could, but her life had turned out differently. She didn't get married when she wanted to, or pregnant when she tried. She had been trying for a number of years, both to get pregnant then to sustain a pregnancy. At the time she started trying to have a baby she was thirty-four years old.

Peg had been born in Kane, Pennsylvania, on February 5, 1950, shortly before the U.S. Navy became involved in the Korean War. Her father, Millard, was a naval officer who had grown up in a large family in rural Mississippi. The Korean War meant that he was gone for the first three years of Peg's life. Still, she describes him as a "huge influence." What was also an influence—though eventually a poignant one—was the enormous love her parents felt and showed for one another throughout their fifty-four years of marriage. Her father would leave notes for his wife on the pillow telling her that he loved her. As a teen, Peg would come home from an evening out to find her parents dancing in each other's arms in the living room or snuggled together in a recliner. "It's everybody's ideal," said Peg. "To have somebody so in love with you that it doesn't go away. It stays and stays and stays." But, she added, there was a good and a bad side to growing up with that ideal as her norm. "How often do you get that?" she asked. "I held that up as my ideal, they didn't argue, they didn't fight and I wanted what they had"—an almost unattainable romantic life.

Peg was the middle of three girls. (The older one, Sandra, was two and a half years older; the younger one, Marie, seven years younger.) With her father gone so much at sea, her mother, also named Margaret, didn't work for the first few years of the girls' lives, although she had been a beautician with her own shop before her marriage.

Margaret came from a family of Catholic immigrants. Her mother had come to America from what is now Croatia; her father from what is now Slovakia. Money was always tight on both sides of the family. Because of the tradition where mothers of young children didn't work, Margaret would take the girls to go and live with her own parents when Millard was at sea. This meant that for the first three or four years of her life, Peg lived with her grandparents. It also meant that as a child she "moved and moved and moved," mostly around the state of Pennsylvania. She went to three different second grades, and by the time she reached high school she had been to sixteen different schools.

Eventually things settled down. Her father retired from the navy after twenty-five years and became a local factory engineer. Her mother also went to work in a lighting factory. The family was now in Ludlow. Peg was twelve years old and in fourth grade. The small town was intensely claustrophobic. "I thought my life was over."

Neither of Peg's parents had finished high school conventionally, though they both did eventually. Her father got his diploma while in the navy. Her mother had dropped out of high school to attend beauty school and didn't get her high school diploma till Peg was in middle school.

The French family had no experience of college. But it was clear that Peg would go. She was bright enough and she wanted to. But she was under the impression that you went to college for vocational purposes rather than to get an education and find out what you might be interested in doing. She knew she wanted to go far away to school, "because I hated this little town that we had moved to." She decided to study marine biology at the University of Miami. But within weeks of arriving in Miami she had dropped all of her science courses when she realized she could study what she liked. She took German, she traced the origins of civilization, and she studied art history. "For me, that is when I fell in love with school." But she had always had what she described as "a life in books," and she began to look for something where she could "continually learn."

From Miami she transferred to George Washington University, then to University of Pittsburgh, where she graduated with a degree in pharmacy.

It was close to where I was living and I chose pharmacy because then I could explain what I was doing. I wanted to be able to justify why I was going to school. I didn't want to be a teacher. That's what all the girls did in my high school. I just wanted something a little bit different. At that time, pharmacy was, for women, a little bit different. I didn't want to do nursing. I just didn't want an absolute traditional female job. So this seemed a compromise.

During her time at Pittsburgh, Peg held down three jobs. She didn't mind. She had always worked—from the time she was a nurse's aide at sixteen. Her jobs were always related to science and medicine. She had a nighttime job in the pharmacy and a weekend job making an IV formula for babies. "Then in my own time I had a third job, which was I grew bacterial colonies for the pharmacy and agar plates. I always thought that if I could work, I should."

Study and practice often go hand in hand in medicine. After receiving her degree, Peg decided she wanted to study pharmacokinetics (the effects that drugs have on us). Again she switched states and enrolled at SUNY–Buffalo for a doctorate in clinical pharmacology. To put herself through graduate school she worked as a pharmacist. She was twenty-nine and still single when she graduated from SUNY. Then while working as a postdoctoral fellow in Hartford, Connecticut, she decided to go for it and become a doctor. Making the decision as she turned thirty was part of a process of evaluating where she was, but more important where she *wasn't* as she entered her thirties. She wasn't married, she wasn't a doctor, she was no longer in her twenties. She had nothing to lose, no real sacrifices to make, and everything to gain.

Why did I go to medical school? I think I thought about it when I was finishing pharmacy. It seemed the pinnacle of what you could do with your knowledge. But I thought it would ruin my life as a woman, because I didn't know if I could have children and be in medical school. My parents loved each other for fifty-four years, and here I was still stumbling along trying to educate myself. I thought I'd meet someone, but I didn't, so I thought I might as well go to medical school.

With the cost of medical school an issue, she applied to Dartmouth in Hanover, New Hampshire. At the time, their program was three years instead of the standard four, "But in between the time I applied and got accepted and went, they extended the program to four years!" Dartmouth's medical school was one of the most prestigious in the country, but Peg wasn't initially in love with it. "It was a lovely little town, but I had a phobia about little towns from my experience in high school." She thought she might transfer somewhere else after a couple of years, but soon after her arrival she fell in love with New England and decided to stay.

In the United States women started going to medical school in solid numbers during the first and middle part of the twentieth century. Harvard Medical School admitted women for the first time in 1945—late, but not as late as Jefferson Medical School in Philadelphia, which finally opened its doors to women in 1960. Even Dartmouth, which had been slow to admit women, both as undergraduates to its college and as graduates to its medical school, eventually came around sometime after Harvard. By 2006 Dartmouth had 4,620 applicants for 82 Med School spots. From those applicants, 36 women and 46 men were accepted.

As soon as she had figured out her professional future, Peg's personal life sorted itself out. In between the time she decided to go to medical school and applied and got accepted, she met a local anesthesiology resident. Once she was up at Dartmouth, the couple bought a condominium together and saw each other on weekends when they could. They both worked weekends, so time was spare.

Being older, being involved with a qualified doctor, and being at a different stage of her life than the other students made Peg feel disconnected from her classmates in medical school. Some of the program was easy, given the work she had done in pharmacology. But the rest of it was tougher than you might imagine. Her basic science studies dated back to Miami, "a long way away." As she put it, there was nothing fresh in her head. Having said that, she was focused and motivated. "In medical school you sort of just do it. You survive. I enjoyed school. I enjoyed learning." I went into medicine as an intellectual endeavor," she said. "For me it was a science." This was why pathology held such appeal when she studied it in her second year. She enjoyed it enough to take it as an elective later. She liked the way pathology tried to make sense of things, and that it got to the intellectual core of medicine, which is the understanding of disease.

Peg did well at medical school and however disconnected she might have felt from her fellow students she had impressed them enough to receive the Good Physician Award—the prize awarded by the graduating class to the student they feel will make the best physician.

In 1983, when she was in her third year of med school, she got married. "My husband wanted a woman with a career; he was always very clear about that. We managed very well when we were both working. It was a very good match. We worked, we traveled, he was very supportive."

When Peg graduated from medical school, she began an internship in internal medicine and promptly entered both the workforce and the trying-to-conceive group. "I was doing my internship after medical school," she recalled, "and trying to get pregnant." At the time Peg was doing her internship, the schedule she was on was much like those described in a highly critical report in the *New England Journal of Medicine* as being of little benefit to either patient or doctor. "I would work thirty-six hours. Sleep for twelve, work for thirty-six, sleep for twelve for a three-week stretch."

Imagine this life. You have a woman who is exhausted, trying to conceive, month after month, without any luck. Every month she faces the disappointment of not being pregnant. Then one time her pregnancy test is positive! But she keeps working around the clock—she has no choice. And then the spotting, the cramping, and the realization that it's over. She tries again. And again. And maybe even again. No babies. Just this intense work pressure that somehow is keeping her from becoming a mother.

If she'd had a real choice, when would have been the best time for her to give birth? Should she have had a baby before, during, or after her training? Should she have been younger and fitter? Or older and more experienced? Each option has its own obvious drawbacks, more to do with a pregnant mother's time and energy levels than its impact on her career. Let's accept that it was harder for Peg to get pregnant when she was exhausted from working so many hours. It might have been easier if she were well rested and unstressed. Let's also assume that it's harder to stay pregnant when you are following a demanding routine. Peg suffered two miscarriages. Did they have anything to do with what was happening at work? She certainly thought so. "I thought maybe if I wasn't working 120 hours a week, it would be easier to get pregnant."

Doctors are notoriously bad patients. Both statistics and anecdotes tell us that women physicians suffer from a high number of complications in their pregnancies—namely preterm labor and delivery—caused by long hours and high stress levels.[6] There are a number of apocryphal stories about women in medicine opting out of giving birth altogether and choosing to adopt their children as one way of dealing with the "problem" of pregnancy. Some doctors' pregnancy stories are heartbreakingly dramatic, particularly the one about the doctor who delivered a baby while she herself was miscarrying. (As she coaxed her patient through her contractions, she felt her own belly contract and she soon began to bleed.) Others are just sad. Like the young pregnant intern who went into preterm labor at twenty-eight weeks after a hectic series of twelve-hour shifts in the emergency room, and felt weak and inferior when she was ordered onto bed rest to save her baby. She realized that schedules would have to be changed to accommodate her and that she would not finish her residency on time. "I remember once hearing an attending scold a young pregnant woman for working too hard," she wrote about her experience. " 'You are with child. This is the most important fact in your life right now. What others expect of you is nothing compared to this.' We as physicians would agree with this advice, but we would never give it to one another."[7]

"I remember I called my chief resident and said that I had had a miscarriage and I needed a day off," said Peg. "And I took a day off and for the other one, I didn't take any time off. I was on call when I started bleeding and when you're on call you have to work. It's sad," she said. "It's sad that you have so little personal time or space for yourself." Women in medicine try to plan the timing of their pregnancies more rigorously than those who think it might be nice to give birth in May or June, for an extra-long maternity/summer break. "Extra long" in a doctor's vocabulary, according to one maternal experience, meant two more days off over Thanksgiving weekend after a son was born in late November.

After her repeated miscarriages, Peg decided to take a break from her chosen career and concentrate on starting her family. Her plan was to leave her medical training for a year. She still wanted to work, but at something less pressured, so she went back to the pathology lab where she had done her medical school elective and took a position as a research assistant.

Pathology is the scientific study of disease. Qualified doctors who become pathologists look at the fluids and tissue of living people to find out why they are sick (or dead when they conduct autopsies). They're the medical detectives. If you have a biopsy, it's a pathologist who will figure out whether the tissue is benign or malignant. Your blood count gets measured by pathologists. As a medical specialty it has one of the longer postgraduate training programs—usually four or five years compared to three for internal medicine or pediatrics—because there is so much to learn. It's generally recognized as a branch of medicine of particular appeal to those with an interest and aptitude in science. Working in the lab didn't mean that Peg had abandoned medicine. This was still valuable experience that would count for something on her résumé. But being a research assistant meant that she had temporaily stepped off the path that led directly to qualifying as a physician.

Peg's life has the kind of twists and turns of a novel. She wants to do something, it doesn't happen, she goes off to do something else and—boom!—she gets what she previously wished for. She wasn't getting pregnant, so she started working in the pathology lab. Then the lab had an opening and offered her a position with them as a pathology resident. She liked the field so she accepted, thus returning to her residency path. And then . . . just a couple of months after beginning her medical residency in pathology, Peg found out she was pregnant.

This pregnancy lasted, but it was difficult. Early on she developed preeclampsia and was put on partial bed rest. This meant she had to cut her residency back to part-time. She worked on a reduced schedule from about the third month, "limping along," as she put it. In addition to her reduced hours she didn't take any calls from the hospital. This was a significant cutback. For pathology residents, taking calls is the most important responsibility. Generally, calls are rotated among all the residents, meaning each resident is on call about once a week or every ten days, and weekends. Whoever is on call is responsible for emergency consultations and problem solving. Being on call means working longer hours, though a number of those can be spent at home, handling matters over the telephone. The problem with losing just one resident in a finite pool of residents means the other residents have to be on call more frequently. In other words, Peg's problematic pregnancy had a direct impact on those around her. They had to work longer hours and more weekends to cover for her. She felt guilty about it. "I decided that I would take a year's worth of calls six months after the baby was born. You don't want to foist your pregnancy on your co-workers. I was supposed to work two and a half days a week, but I always did more—maybe about three. It seemed to be fine."

Then Aaron was born. His first Apgar scores were a low 2 out of 10. And in fact he needed to be resuscitated. The umbilical cord had been wrapped around his neck twice. He wasn't a C-section, but he was a mid-forceps delivery, and he was in the neonatal intensive care unit for a couple of days. "It was a trauma," said Peg. "Coming out of that I was supposed to have eight weeks off, but at the end of eight weeks I didn't want to go back. So I asked for another month and I got it. Then I went back full-time."

Peg had an au pair, who had moved in before Aaron was born so "that was all okay—she knew what to do." Peg wanted to keep nursing, which was hard; she pumped her breast milk regularly and "had to organize things around that." She was fortunate that she worked in a hospital with an obstetrics floor and a comfortable nursing center where she could go and pump in comfort.

For six months she worked full-time, but there was one huge complication that many mothers can relate to. Aaron was a baby who didn't sleep. He was waking up three times a night, and she was working full-time the next day. She was exhausted. "I was so tired, I would dream about sleep when I was asleep." Her pediatrician's credo was that for the first six months babies had to be responded to when they cried. She wasn't to let Aaron cry; he needed to be picked up and soothed. Peg became the sole nighttime soother—a situation that might be familiar to many women.

How many mothers quit work because they are too tired? Peg didn't want to quit; she thought if she cut back her hours she might manage. Dropping with exhaustion, she asked if she could continue her residency part-time. Her request was denied. "It was nothing personal," said Peg.

No one thought she would actually lose her job. But she did. The problem was that the matching program that the department relied on was already full. I had been a very good resident," said Peg. "I was elected to an honors society. But there was no mechanism for a part-time resident in the pathology department. They didn't know how to schedule it. The system didn't allow for it."

If you've ever looked for flexibility in your job without success, you can probably relate to Peg's misfortune. Asking an employer to allow you to cut back from full- to part-time is a tricky prospect, as it allows a company to reexamine, and perhaps redefine, your job. As Peg found out, this does not always work to your advantage. Peg is the only mother in this book who was let go by her employers because of a desire for flexibility. She did not become a stay-at-home mother out of choice. She wanted what the trend in medicine was advocating—a part-time situation. Her story gives us an insight into the wide gap between the theory and the practice of maternal policies. If women are told to look for part-time work, then part-time work should be available to them.

Actually, Peg was offered work in other specialties. She was offered part-time residencies in pediatrics and anesthesiology, and a full-time residency in radiology. The offers were flattering, but the specialties held little appeal. "I didn't want to be those things," she said. "I wanted to be a pathologist." It was a tough lesson to learn that her earlier fear that she might not be able to combine medicine and motherhood had been valid.

So here were two doctors, married to each other, who had recently become parents. Parenthood caused one doctor to be spectacularly derailed from her career and left her exhausted and confused. The other was . . . fine.

If this turn of events leaves you shocked but not surprised, I'll just quickly mention the 1999 study, "When Doctors Marry Doctors."[8] The study found that "Compared with female physicians who were not married to other physicians, women in dual-doctor families more often reported substantial limitations in professional life for family reasons." Such limitations, the report continued, "were rarely reported by male physicians."

Peg's juggling act actually had less to do with her husband's profession than with the requirements medicine imposed on her as she tried to have a family.

> Medicine—you are supposed to commit your life to it. I think the attitude is still there, although it has changed a lot. It's still there and that's why they are called residents; I mean, they were supposed to live at the hospital, they resided there. That was supposed to be your life, and that's how you learn medicine— just by overwhelming yourself in it for a period of time in your life—and I couldn't jump into it the same way a young single person could. Once you have a family and try to do something like medicine, it becomes a struggle, a juggling act.

"Can one be a successful physician (academic or otherwise) and still be a 'good' parent?" asked Ellen S. More in her book *Restoring the Balance: Women Physicians and the Profession of Medicine, 1850-1995*.[9] "To some extent the answer depends on the values of the institution where one works." More wrote that "as a culture we do not seem to have internalized the message that men are parents, too." That message—that reality—didn't seem to have been internalized by those in Peg's orbit. The message Peg got from both work and home was that she was a mother. At the same time, she got the message that her needs or even her choices as a mother made her of little enough value as a doctor to be let go.

Initially, Peg felt a huge relief that she no longer had to juggle. She had a few months at home, then the medical school approached her to teach a seminar and tutor a group. She accepted their offer, seeing it as a short-term part-time solution. A year later she had her second child, Annie. With a son and a daughter to take care of, she decided to focus on her family completely. She had a successful husband, she was about to turn forty, and she decided to do nothing. Or as she put it, "*Nothing*!"

I'm often struck by how we view our time at home. The Play-Doh, the coloring, the swings, the ball games, the meals, the endless chores—all of this adds up to *Nothing*? Of course it doesn't. You don't think Peg literally did nothing all day long. But you can understand—as I can—why she describes her time in that way. Nothing she did was validated. "I took care of two little kids full time," she said, laughing at the memory as she described building sandcastles in the summer and snowmen in the winter, feeding and changing her children, volunteering at their nursery school and helping out at the local co-op grocery with her baby daughter on her back. "Until you've been through it, you don't know what's involved."

Being deprived of the opportunity to at least try to make a career as a doctor left her angry at the system. It never occurred to her that she would do nothing (*Nothing*!) forever. What was less clear, though, was whether she would ever get to be a doctor. She felt that something had gone from her life. Some part of her identity was missing and she noticed the loss.

For a couple of years Peg's schedule revolved entirely around her children. Many mothers can find this kind of daily structure overwhelming, but for women coming from endless days in the hospital, it's a comfortable adjustment. Hanover is a tiny, relaxed, and friendly place where everybody knows everybody. Peg loved the time she spent with Aaron and Annie. She loved being a mom. She had a "really good time" being very involved in her children's lives. And as time passed, the unpleasantness of her departure from the hospital receded.

When Annie was in preschool, Peg was ready to go back to work. For a while she just tutored part-time through the medical school. But once Annie was in kindergarten and at school all day long, Peg joined the medical school staff and began training other people to become the doctor she herself wanted to be. For now she ignored that particular irony and just enjoyed working. She found that teaching and being a mother was an effortless combination.

> In that respect, absolutely it was much easier; the child care was much easier. I think that's why I went back to work when I did. I knew they were at school for most of the day, well taken care of, doing what they had to do. So you know there was a reason I waited until they were at school until I went back. The child care becomes much easier when there is school full-time. I don't think I could have done it—I couldn't do it—when Aaron was a baby. I wanted to work part-time and not full-time for that reason. It was unsettling for me to have a little baby and not be there with him.

To Peg, teaching at the medical school was a job, not a career. In many ways it was a good life. She had the summers off to be with her kids. When a friend and co-worker asked her to consider a tenure track position in the anatomy department she realized she was on the wrong path. She didn't want to teach medicine, she wanted to practice it. In order to resume her residency, which was what she realized she wanted, she had to go back to the department she had left and reapply. She interviewed and was accepted back—but she had to wait a year for the residency to start. During that time she was forced to confront the fact that her marriage wasn't working. The romantic ideal her parents had enjoyed was not hers. The realization that she would probably get divorced had been part of the impetus to resume her residency. A resident would earn more than a medical school teacher and Peg was beginning to plan for a financially independent future. "By that time the paths we had taken were so different," was Peg's comment on the end of her marriage. "I think for two people to stay together you have to grow together and we had grown apart by doing such different things in our lives."

I did not want to explore the reasons for the divorce or try to find out who was at fault. That is not the point of this story.

Peg restarted her pathology residency in July 1998 at the age of forty-eight after a ten-year break. She was in peak physical condition, as she had taken up running. Six months later she separated from her husband. It goes without saying this was a traumatic time. The next four years were the toughest of her life.

To add to the load, her father was dying of cancer. Any free block of time she got, she would use to visit him, a ten-hour drive away. She was working full-time and had to take care of two young children who were now living in two homes. This is not the fairy-tale moment of a comeback you might be dreaming of. This was a hard life. She couldn't sleep, she couldn't eat (she lost twenty-two pounds). She was extremely anxious about money. She did not want to be financially dependent on her ex-husband for the rest of her life. Both practically and psychologically she knew that she needed to make money of her own. She couldn't afford the slightest glitch in her child-care plans. She had mountains of studying to do, exams to take and pass. "You know if I had really thought about the details of all of this, I would have felt so overwhelmed, so out of place, so I didn't," she said when I asked her how she managed. But she didn't think about whether or not she could do it, she focused on the fact that she *wanted* to do it.

She worked out a custody agreement that actually made things a little easier. She and her ex-husband divided the week in two. The kids' summers were spent at camp, vacations were split between the two households. During the school year, when her ex-husband took the children every few days, she had a chunk of time when she got a break. Peg's life would have been much harder if she had been the custodial parent, as many divorced mothers are. Many children of divorce live with their mothers and spend one evening a week and every other weekend with their fathers. The idea is that children benefit from having one home. If Peg had had this arrangement, she might not have been able to continue her residency.

Her friends carried her through, and she continued to express enormous gratitude to them fifteen years later. One of her co-workers, a good friend, would buy her food and bring it into work. Another told her she could call anytime, even in the middle of the night. At one point Peg, who was lying awake in bed panicking about money, took her friend up on the offer and called. The woman who had told her to call had been through the same thing, and Peg found her immensely reassuring. "I can't remember much of what she said, but it calmed me down."

For the most part, Peg got through this period trying not to think about her future. "I didn't let myself think about that. In terms of the work, it was a huge adjustment having to get two kids and myself ready for work every morning. My work was completely tainted by the fact I had to get out the door at a certain time to go and pick up the kids, or I couldn't come into work any earlier because I had to take the kids to school. Some of that is just a factor of being a single parent, and some of it is a factor of being older and having kids."

As any working mother knows, it is not the school day that is the problem, it is what happens after school. If your child has activities that he needs to be transported to, someone has to provide the transport. Peg recognized that she was lucky that she could solve this problem by leaving the kids where they were in an after-school program.

They could go to the after-school program at the same elementary school where they went to school. And then when my son was in middle school, he actually worked at the same after-school program that he had been in when he was at elementary school. He didn't get paid or anything, but they really liked him and he helped. The fact that I physically didn't need to leave work and transport them or hire somebody to pick them up and take them home or take them to a babysitter after school was huge for me.

Still, it wasn't that easy. Again Peg relied on her friends to help.

My daughter did gymnastics after school and she would go to her best friend's house, and my friend Mary would watch her, feed her an after-school snack, and run the girls to gymnastics, and I would pick them up because that helped Mary. She had four kids, and she would be getting dinner and everything like that. She had a little one. So we helped each other out. That was another piece that made it work, the fact that I could trade time and rides with people.

Peg's responsibilities were almost neatly divided in two. On the one hand, children; on the other, work. It was a seesaw that provided its own kind of balance to her life. Being a single mother meant she no longer had the support of a spouse with the children at home; on the other hand, her children were with their father for half the week, and during those days she had only herself to take care of. Then she could concentrate solely on her job, and that was "a huge relief." Mornings, for example, were so much easier. She didn't have to get three people out the door.

I still got up at the same time, but it just—I didn't have all of the organization that starts the evening before. It just freed that up. It didn't feel so much like *time* more than the stress and energy that were gone. It wasn't an abundance of time that I had. And in the evening I could stay there and work. I didn't get up from my desk and walk out the door when there was still work that I needed to do or wanted to do. I didn't just leave because I had to take care of the kids.

This made the time that she did have with the children something she could enjoy. On those days work could take a (comparative) backseat, and the children became her priority. The ebb and flow of intensity was now spread over a week rather than a single day. Although the days when she had to juggle both work and family single-handed could be overwhelming, the pattern settled into something manageable. There is no question that she felt—and continues to feel—guilt and sadness that she "deprived" her children of a childhood with two married parents. Yet as she looked back with a sense of perspective gained by time she realized that while her kids didn't have a storybook family as such, she gave them something she herself hadn't had as a child—stability. "Even though their father and I were divorced, their life changed so little," she said. "Their friends were still their friends." Going back and forth from one household to another only involved traveling less than half a mile. They never changed schools or had to make new friends. They remained in the same environment from birth until college.

As she navigated her new life, Hanover's small-town size worked to her advantage. Driving distances were short. Everyone and everything were minutes away. She could—and did—jump in her car and race to where she was going, counting the fractions of miles on her odometer. ("Three miles from the hospital, a mile and a quarter from the middle school and the high school, and about a mile and a half from the elementary school. Gymnastics was three miles.") Naturally, Aaron and Annie hated it if she was late. "I remember the anxiety of driving too fast. They would be moody when I picked them up."

Peg wanted to work and make a decent enough salary so that she wouldn't be financially dependent on her ex-husband. Within a couple of years she was making enough money to forgo alimony. In her first year as a resident she earned $44,000, ten years later she was up to $180,000. Divorce is a reality that sometimes propels women to a comeback against their will. They have to work—they need the money. The financial beating mothers get when their family is split in two has been well documented. If you have to work after a divorce, should you be thinking short-term or long-term? Do you want a job or a career? With bills piling up, do you even have the luxury of that choice? The financial impact of divorce on your social security benefits, medical insurance, living arrangements, vacations, hobbies, and mental health can be devastating.

A study conducted by the California Career Services a few years ago described the "walking wounded" of divorce, dealing with fear, anxiety, depression, and anger, and being emotionally unready to make solid career choices. "However," the study reported, "the further the partners are from separation, the more ready they are to consider career issues."[10]

The California study reported that women who are forced to join the workforce because of divorce are often riddled with anxiety about their futures and their job-related skills. They are guilty and worried about their children, and they face the pressure of finding additional child care while they work. The study recommended that women find career counselors to help them break down seemingly insurmountable tasks into manageable steps.

Peg had a career waiting to be resumed, and she knew what she wanted to do. She had a custodial arrangement that made her situation a little easier. This doesn't mean her life was easy. The period she described sounded harrowing in the extreme, possibly the worst time of her life. Yes, there are women who are worse off than she was. There are women who have worse divorces and are in more precarious financial situations than hers. And as we have seen, even non-divorcing women who *choose* to rejoin the workforce can be anxious about their skills and guilty about leaving their children with other caregivers.

Peg struggled, but she got through it. After about a year, when she was beginning to get used to her routine, a younger doctor came to the department to begin her pathology residency. She, too, was a single mother. Her son was three years old. The first night that this new resident was on call, her babysitter telephoned to say she was sick and couldn't work. The younger doctor had to leave to go home and take care of her son while the other residents filled in and took her calls. "I remember talking to her and saying, 'You can't just have plan A, you need to have plan A, B, C, and D,'" said Peg. "I had that. I had another layer of friends and then the next layer of friends that I could go to. Everybody helped out. Things would come up at work where I couldn't leave. I would be sent frozen tissue and would be cutting it to prepare it for slides. I couldn't just leave. But these were people I had known for twenty years. If they were picking up their kids, they would pick mine up."

Still, women with families who are already leading second-shift lives with their jobs and their child and home care find that in medicine they have a third shift of plowing through textbooks. For some time, until his death in 2001, Peg had an extra shift of going to visit her sick father. When her children were with their father, Peg would jump in her car, drive ten hours, and spend her "free" time with her dad. It didn't leave much time for reading. But there are medical books on tape, and over the years she resorted to those, studying as she drove.

It wasn't enough. She was lucky that her pathology department had a strong enough program in clinical pathology (the study of fluid analysis) that she could pass her medical board exams without studying. But she didn't pass the anatomic (tissue analysis) pathology boards. She was able to get a job as a pathologist while retaking the anatomic boards, but she spent a year of her extra time studying again. The kids had their homework. She had hers.

In 2002 she finished her residency at Dartmouth-Hitchcock. She wanted to continue giving her children stability so she was determined to find a job locally. There no openings in pathology at Dartmouth, which caused her a minor panic, but then right at the end of her training she learned there was one job going in the area—at the

VA Hospital—about six miles from her house. She applied for the position and got it. She could stay put.

As the children got older, the juggling act got easier, but not much. Now she would try to run out of the VA Hospital to get to their concerts at school, or go to their plays, or make it to their after-school sports activities. She describes this period as "a different struggle."

Back in 1915 another doctor, Dr. Anna Fullerton, had almost exactly predicted this struggle. "If she would excel in her profession, she would live a lonely life," she wrote in her diary about a hypothetical doctor. "And carry a double burden—her professional and her household cares also in most cases. Whereas the man may have a help-mate to share his joys and his sorrows and to make his home a harbor of rest after toil, the woman must do without this close companionship . . . a woman cannot undertake the duties of wife and mother and at the same time give herself as she should to the demands of a life so strenuous both mentally and physically."[11]

Eventually Aaron learned to drive, and things really changed—now he could help. He was able to pick up his sister and run to the store for milk. "The layers of complexity of trying to work and have kids," Peg said, "they get lifted as they get older and become more independent." And finally, "All of it came together for me and made it doable," said Peg.

Peg's comeback took several years of struggle. Still, by the time her kids were finishing school, she had set up a well-organized, manageable lifestyle. Peg had a job in the pathology lab at the Veterans Hospital where she worked five days a week from 8:00 until 5:00 with a short half-hour break for lunch. Her days were busy, but she was able to pick up the phone and call home to check in. She took calls one week out of two months. During that time, calls would come in from 5:00 p.m. to 8:00 a.m. Sometimes she might take as many as ten to fifteen; other days there would be none. Roughly once a week in that time, she would have to go in to the hospital.

At work her schedule was varied. One week she would do anatomic pathology; the next, clinical. While on anatomic pathology she would look at specimens that came in from surgery and analyze them. She'd look at bladders, kidneys, or colons—anything that came in from the operating room—and dictate notes. During the weeks she worked in clinical pathology, her work was more chemistry and microbiology. She'd deal with the blood bank, all the bone marrows and the smears, and also what are called FNAs—fine needle aspirations. In today's medicine, biopsies are taken from inside the body with long needles as part of noninvasive surgery. You might be asked to swallow an endoscopy tube with a tiny fiber-optic needle on its end. In this way your esophagus or stomach, lymph nodes or duodenum can be examined with ultrasound. Peg would be the doctor performing this procedure. When Peg looked at a slide or searched for something in an image on a computer, this became her sole focus. There was no conflict; she was completely engrossed with her job.

Outside of this world she had made a life. She had a horse that she loved to ride. She joined a chorus. She dated. Aaron was at Boston University, Annie was a senior in high school. She got to read, both medical and nonmedical books. She even had time to attend medical conferences, which she loved. She found the few days away from the office—in the company of colleagues she liked and admired, learning about the most cutting-edge innovations in her field—energizing and enjoyable.

It was a long and complicated journey, planned and unplanned. There is no end in sight to this late-starting career. Why should there be? "I got my first real job at the age of fifty-two," she said laughing. What advice would she have given the young Peg? I asked her. "I would have gone to medical school sooner than I did," she said. "In retrospect I should have had the confidence, I should have believed that it wouldn't distort my life. Other than that there is nothing I would have changed. Look at what I have now. I have all that I wanted. I have my job as a physician. I have my kids. I can support myself, I can go off and do these crazy things like have voice lessons and ride my horse. It was a struggle. And at the end of the day it was absolutely worth it. Would I love to be in a great relationship? Absolutely. But my happiness doesn't revolve around that."

Elaine Stone

To have that sense of one's intrinsic worth which consti-
tutes self-respect is potentially to have everything.

Joan Didion

ELAINE STONE IS a partner at the international corporate law firm of
Covington & Burling in Washington, D.C. She is married to a rabbi
and is the mother of three children. By anyone's standards, Elaine's
comeback has been spectacular. She joined Covington after five years
of staying at home full-time and made partner within five years.
Elaine didn't quit her career on the birth of her first child, nor on the
birth of her second. She worked hard combining motherhood and
work for more than a decade. It wasn't until her third child was born
that she quit. When she eventually went back to work, she made the
connection to Covington in the same way that I found her—through
a parent at her son's school.

   Women who have spent several years at home and are looking to
reenter the workforce are constantly told to "network, network, network," as an article in *More* magazine on the subject put it. Telling
mothers to network is a bit like telling them to breathe. We do it all
the time and without thinking. How did you find your pediatrician?

Your realtor? Your kids' summer camp or school? How did you join your book club? Get the name of your divorce lawyer? Hire your babysitter? Mothers tend to operate on a word-of-mouth referral service. And once our children are at school, we have an immediate and extensive source of information and contacts. The parents of our kids' friends become our friends. We know more about each other than we probably should. And we help each other out.

Elaine Stone got to know former Clinton special counsel Lanny Breuer because she looks exactly like his wife. The resemblance is uncanny. Both women are slight with short dark curls that frame angular faces. They have intelligent, humorous brown eyes with gazes that don't seem to miss a trick. I've never met Nancy Breuer (who's also a lawyer), but when I went into Lanny's office at Covington to talk to him about Elaine, I got a frisson of shock. I thought he had Elaine Stone's photographs all over his walls. I knew he was her friend and mentor, but this seemed to be taking it a little far!

Teachers at their sons' school often made the same mistake. The two mothers were mistaken for each other more than once, especially during the first year when their sons were actually classmates. The families were bound to become friendly.

Not many women looking to return to law have the advantage of getting to know a senior partner at a prestigious law firm because they look like his wife. Elaine's strength lay in being able to pursue the connection. When you know her history you'll understand why.

She was born Elaine Wintroub in 1953, the same year that Simone de Beauvoir's book *The Second Sex* was published in the United States.[1] The book redefined the idea of motherhood. Women were told that they shouldn't consider having children an absolute goal. Motherhood was just one aspect of their identity as women. "The mother's relation with her children takes form within the totality of her life; it depends upon her relations with her husband, her past, her occupation, herself," wrote de Beauvoir. (The year 1953 was also when *Playboy* magazine first hit the newsstands—just to keep things in perspective.)

Like most of the women you have read about, Elaine was not born into the world she came to inhabit. She did not come from a long line of high-powered East Coast attorneys; her family was a respectable, middle-class Conservative Jewish one that lived in Omaha, Nebraska. Elaine was the "very much wanted, not planned" youngest daughter of a local businessman and his enormously capable stay-at-home wife. Her two older brothers, Bob and David, were respectively sixteen years and twelve years her senior.

The family was a close one, despite the large age gaps. Bob, who subsequently became a doctor, left home to go to the University of Michigan when Elaine was two, but he decided to return to Omaha for medical school specifically so that he could be near his little sister. Still, her much older brothers had their own lives to lead, and she essentially grew up as an only child—the youngest child of two middle-aged parents. Her mother, Eve, was forty when she was born; her father, Lou, was forty-five. His heart attack when Elaine was fifteen made her worry about the health of her parents for the remainder of her childhood.

Lou Wintroub was a quiet, witty, intelligent man with a sardonic sense of humor, who worked extremely hard as the comptroller in a family-owned air-conditioning business. Elaine described him as a man with an unassailable sense of honesty. He was also kind and decent, and Elaine's recollection of his influence was that she absorbed his qualities by osmosis. "My dad wasn't rigid or harsh with me. The lines were clear; he was slow to anger."

Her memories of growing up are of a simpler America, where girls ate raisins, played cards, and picked dandelions with their dads. "My father used to sing one particular mournful song, 'Let's Saddle Old Paint for the Last Time and Ride,' when he tucked me in when I was little," Elaine remembered. It was a time, as described by Robert L. Griswold in *Fatherhood in America: A History,* when fathers were seen primarily as breadwinners in an increasingly consumer-oriented society.[2] According to Griswold, fathers "helped out" their wives with daily household care but did little sustained childhood maintenance. Like Lou, they were friends and guides to their children, role models rather than voices of parental infallibility.

While Lou was a gentle presence, his wife, Eve, was much more vibrant. She adored her only daughter and tried to give her everything she needed. She reminisced about bringing up Elaine when I went to see her in February 2006, three months before she died at the age of ninety-three. By then she had had some serious setbacks with her health and was living in a sunny assisted-care facility a block from the ocean in Santa Monica, California. She was vivacious and funny, sharp as a tack. Even then, moving (fairly speedily, it has to be said) around the building clutching her walker, she kept up a nonstop stream of chatter as her eyes darted quickly about behind thick glasses. In conversation she never missed a point or a beat unless she hadn't heard me properly. When she didn't catch a question, she wasn't shy about asking me to speak up, and she did so with great charm.

"She has been a joy since she was conceived," she said of Elaine. "It was the easiest pregnancy and the easiest delivery." I asked her where she thought Elaine got her drive. "Her father," she replied immediately. "He never let anything interfere with his work. He was very single-minded."

As a young girl Elaine found both schoolwork and school life easy. But in middle school she became self-conscious and shy. When her mother noticed this, she found Elaine a drama teacher to help her gain confidence. Once a week Elaine would go for a lesson, during which she would act out long poems and scenes. "It was this way I found my voice," Elaine said. It also gave her a love of drama that she carried through her adult life. She was an enthusiastic amateur playwright and actress, from acting in plays in high school, where she won an award for best actress, to taking part in theatrical workshops at Esalen, where she began traveling for vacations in middle age.

Broadly speaking, if her father was responsible for her single-mindedness, her mother gave Elaine confidence. Her intelligence was her own. She did well enough in high school to get into Brandeis and after graduation she prepared to head east.

It was 1971, the year that Women's Equality Day was established by an act of Congress and an episode of *All in the Family* had Gloria Stivic discovering women's lib. Kate Millett's *Sexual Politics* had come out the year before.[3] Writing that "women are at the bottom unless they sleep with the top," Millett was a militant who pushed for nothing short of a feminist revolution. Women should no longer accept their "oppression," she said. Women's liberation was the message of the day, particularly for female undergraduates living independent lives for the first time.

Brandeis was a progressive place at whose core lay a commitment to Judaism. Named after the late Supreme Court justice Louis Brandeis, it was—and is—the only nonsectarian Jewish-sponsored university in the country. From the time it was founded in 1948 it was co-ed, always stressing both social justice and academic excellence. The school also had a good drama department. It was an attractive choice for Elaine, who as a teenager had been an enthusiastic member of the United Synagogue Youth, a conservative social and volunteer organization. "Judaism was my zone growing up. We kept kosher in the house. I regularly attended services. It was always very tied up in my social world."

Brandeis was where Elaine met Warren Stone, her future husband and the future rabbi. The university had been an obvious choice for him, too. He had come there from a sophisticated, cultured suburban Boston family. Having rebelled strongly against his religion from the time of his bar mitzvah, Warren reconnected to his Judaism while studying international relations on a fellowship in Jerusalem. By the time he met Elaine, he had already begun to believe that he had a mission to serve, though he wasn't entirely certain where it would lead him. She was a freshman. He was in his senior year majoring in Near Eastern studies and Judaica, deciding whether or not to begin rabbinical studies.

The couple met during a lecture given by Rabbi Mordecai Kaplan, the cofounder of the Young Israel Modern Orthodox movement (whose daughter, Judith, had been the first woman to become bat mitzvah after her father thought of the idea the day before). Both had previously noticed the other on campus and had felt drawn to a "presence" (Warren) and someone who was "*so* cute" (Elaine).

The lecture took place on the evening of Simchat Torah, when the scrolls of the Torah are removed from the ark and rolled. It was Warren's job that night to roll the scrolls, and he picked Elaine to do it with him. Scroll rollers symbolize a bride and her groom. "There was a sparkle, a depth, a beauty," said Warren, recalling his first impressions of his future wife. "She was honest, genuine, capable, intelligent. She had a goodness and a sense of ethics."

"I had this feeling of exhilaration, of running across the lawn," said Elaine. "He was very good looking and very tanned. He had a creative energy that was in him."

Warren Stone *is* a good-looking man. He has dark, slightly graying hair with a year-round tan and a large smile that reveals the perfectly even, white teeth of the son of a dental specialist (which his father was). He dresses casually but neatly, with well-pressed jeans, nice shirts. He is warm and accessible, a little reserved.

The first time I met him in his sunny office at the temple he runs in Kensington, Maryland, I was struck not so much by his creative energy—and this is a man who ice-skates every morning, who drums and dances, who is an enthusiastic photographer, who has music constantly playing—but by his absorption in all things spiritual. Warren thinks about the meaning of life *all the time*. Thinking isn't a passive exercise. He reads about it, he talks about it; he studies it and writes about it. Understanding the meaning of life is the meaning of his own life.

The lawyer and the rabbi. It sounds like it's meant to be a joke: *Have you heard the one about the lawyer and the rabbi?* The reality is a modern, liberated dual-career couple navigating a culture where the wife traditionally has a supporting role to play in her husband's career. Elaine didn't need to have her own career; she could have found a fulfilling place in Warren's world. Yet she had her own aspirations to follow. While pursuing their own professional interests, the Stones produced three thriving, successful children. Their two daughters are on their way to graduate schools; their son is in high school. How did they make it work?

In *The Rabbi's Wife*, Shuly Rubin Schwartz explains that the American rabbinate was —for most of the twentieth century—a two-person career.[4] In this world the wife had more than a role to play. According to Schwartz, many wives (though not all) had considered this a good thing. They had been able to get the experience of working outside the home through their husbands' jobs. But Elaine never saw her identity in this light. "From the time Warren was a rabbi, I had another job," she said.

Her professional independence was absolute—completely separate from her husband's, although she was a devoted and supportive member of his congregation. "Warren's congregation has always been part of my life," she said. "It has been the main fulcrum, no question that it has affected my life distinctly. In a positive way. Throughout it has been the fulcrum about which our lives have turned. We have gotten emotional sustenance from it."

Yet as a professional place it has always been his congregation, not theirs. She has contributed, of course. She regularly taught Sunday school, and once wrote and produced a play with the congregants at his temple. But she always knew there was much more she could have done. "You could be there all the time, you could teach in the schools, visit other homes. You could help make food for the congregational events and parties."

From the start of her relationship with Warren, Elaine felt liberated enough to lead her own life. The atmosphere of the early 1970s made her future husband as enlightened as she was. He believed just as firmly in her equality as she did. Early on the two established a pattern of academic and professional give-and-take that would continue over the next thirty years. The giving part involved some significant sacrifices on each side—there were jobs not taken, jobs that were left, moves from state to state. But Warren and Elaine's idea of charity—or love, or service—began at home. And that was how they chose to live together.

A few months after their relationship began they moved to New York so that Warren could study with Abraham Joshua Heschel, the professor of Jewish ethics and mysticism at the Jewish Theological Seminary of America in New York. Elaine transferred down to Barnard College and went with him. One year later, in 1973, they left New York for Israel, where Elaine spent her junior year and Warren enrolled at the Hebrew University of Jerusalem. During the upheaval they made three decisions: one religious, Warren moved from the Conservative to the Reform movement; one academic, Elaine chose anthropology as her major; and one romantic, they decided to get married.

When Elaine graduated from Barnard, it was time for her career to determine their next move. She had decided to go to law school and wanted to move to the West Coast. Her parents and brothers had left Nebraska and settled in Los Angeles, and she wanted to be near them. Warren was able to transfer his rabbinical school to the West Coast for one year—but only one year. In order to graduate, he would have to return to New York. This meant they went to Los Angeles for one year, Elaine went to UCLA Law School, then she transferred to New York University. By 1978 they had had moved five times in seven years. Seven years of studying for professions they were finally ready to begin. They had no interest in becoming parents yet. It was time to start work.

What was it like for a woman hoping to become a lawyer thirty years ago? In the sixties law firms had been blatantly unenthusiastic about hiring women, fearing that children and families would make them unproductive and unreliable. Some had even posted "No Women" notices on the sign-up sheets for interviews at law schools. But by the end of the seventies the law was no longer on the law firms' side. The Civil Rights Act forbidding sex discrimination had been passed in 1964. In 1975 the Supreme Court had ruled that it was unconstitutional for states to deny women equal opportunity for jury service. And in 1978 Congress passed the Pregnancy Discrimination Act, which reversed two earlier Supreme Court decisions that had denied "pregnant people" disability benefits, and women the use of sick leave during childbirth.

In their 1986 book, *Where They Are Now: The Story of the Women of Harvard Law 1974,* Jill Abramson and Barbara Franklin wrote that in 1974, for the first time in any Harvard Law School class, "more women than men went to work at large elite firms."[5] The authors pointed out that the improvement came as a result of a number of sex-discrimination suits filed against some of the nation's most prestigious law firms, "challenging the firms' dismal records in hiring and promoting qualified women." The suits were eventually settled, and firms pledged to increase the number of women in their ranks.

Elaine had done extremely well in law school, despite the disruption of the move. She had been an editor on law review and a member of the honor society Order of the Coif. She wanted to pursue a judicial clerkship before applying to a law firm. This was not an unusual choice. Clerks had interesting lives, and clerkships were great entries on a legal résumé. Meanwhile, Warren was looking for an entry-level job as assistant rabbi in a large congregation. The couple decided there were four cities across the country they liked where both of them might find what they were looking for: Boston; Los Angeles; Washington, D.C.; and San Francisco. Together they began to apply for jobs in each city.

Elaine got the first offer—a clerkship with Frank Coffin, then chief justice of the U.S. Court of Appeals for the First Circuit, whose court was in Boston. It sounded perfect. But there was one drawback. Coffin's court might have been in Boston, but his chambers (and Elaine's office) were miles away in Portland, Maine. There wasn't a single Reform congregation in Maine at that time. But Warren agreed that Elaine should take this clerkship. So he stopped looking for a position for himself, and for the year of her clerkship he went back to school again, receiving a DMin (Doctor of Ministry) in family counseling. When the clerkship ended, after almost a decade together, the couple had two jobs. Warren became assistant rabbi at the large, prominent temple of Stephen S. Wise in Los Angeles while Elaine found a job as an associate at what was then a small boutique law firm, Munger, Tolles & Rickershauser. Today it is much larger and it is now Munger, Tolles & Olson.

She was twenty-six; he was almost thirty. It was 1979 and they were back in Los Angeles near Elaine's family. They were both working hard, but they were settled. All the big decisions had been made. But in 1980, less than a year after the move, both Warren's mother and brother suddenly died, and the double loss left Warren and Elaine feeling it was "time to affirm life," as Elaine put it. They decided to have a baby. Nomi was born on February 14, 1981, a Valentine's child.

There was no question of Elaine quitting her job to become a full-time mother. She had worked too hard and for too long to get to where she was—and they needed her salary. From the time she joined a law firm Elaine outearned her husband. As Munger, Tolles had no formal maternity leave policy, Elaine had actually drafted a version of one (not too different from what's typical today) before she gave birth. She had given herself three months' paid leave, in line with what other law firms were beginning to offer as official policy.

The vast sprawl of Los Angeles makes it a tough city for commuters. Returning to work after her maternity leave marked the start of a period of lengthy stressful driving. Elaine immediately felt torn between work and home. As she drove home after her first day back at the office, she was stopped for speeding. She tried to explain to the police officer that she was rushing back to her baby. His response was that a child might be better off with a mother who was actually alive.

After Nomi was born Elaine sensed she had taken a step off the career fast track. It was hard to be single-minded about work when she was emotionally divided between the law firm and home. She was less inclined to work long hours. The firm was flexible and supportive, but she had cut back to hours she described as "less than full-time," which in her world meant a nine to five rather than a nine to seven or nine to nine day. She was experiencing some of the misery well known to mothers who work long hours in offices far from where they live. Driving each day from the San Fernando Valley to downtown Los Angeles and back again, she always felt torn. She wanted to be at home more than she was able to be. No matter where she was—home or office—she thought she should be in the other place. She loved the law firm and she loved her work, but the realization that having a small child was making her climb up the ladder more challenging led her to reevaluate her professional future.

In order to work the hours she did, she had to have help. Her first babysitter stole from her and then disappeared, an unpleasant and unsettling experience. Her parents were close, but at a forty-five-minute drive away, not close enough to be a daily resource. Meanwhile, Warren, who described himself as "moderately hands-on for the first child," was making his way as the assistant rabbi at his large congregation. So his time was limited, too. The couple barely saw each other. They were finding it hard to raise a child under these circumstances, and harder to have a real relationship together.

Within a year of Nomi's birth they decided to move to a smaller city. By now they had both been in their respective jobs for three years, a decent enough stretch. This time it was Warren's turn to choose where they settled. He looked for a place where he could have his own pulpit; he wanted to live on the coast. On a beautiful stretch of water in Corpus Christi, Texas, in a tiny community of only a couple of hundred people, he found what he was looking for. In a leap of faith the couple sold their house, packed up their toddler, and moved.

The move meant that Elaine was forced to stop work temporarily. But she was optimistic. The commuting would end and they would live a simpler, less frenetic life in a smaller community, where the people were friendly and welcoming. She would find herself a job just as soon as the family was settled. Her optimism began to falter when the adjustment turned out to be much tougher than she had anticipated. The cultural change was apparent as they drove to Corpus Christi from the airport in San Antonio. They passed ranch after ranch after ranch all the way down the highway with nothing in between. At one point they stopped for lunch and Warren asked for a tuna fish sandwich. He was met with a blank stare. Tuna fish? Unheard of in this world.

They arrived in Texas in the heat of summer. It was overwhelmingly oppressive. Elaine had to learn she couldn't go grocery shopping in the middle of the day—it was too hot to leave the house. She felt isolated and gloomy. She had no friends, and though her new community reached out to her, she felt uncomfortable. After all, they were all her husband's congregants. Like many women who stop work and become full-time mothers, the contrast between her two lives was stark. Before, she had been constantly rushed. Now, she was stuck at home alone with a small child in a strange place. "Being at home with a young child—I didn't know how to do it," she remembered. "I had never done it. I didn't have a pattern; I didn't have connections yet—I didn't know any mothers with young children. It was hard."

She wanted to find friends independently of the congregation, and she definitely wanted to work. But in order to find a job in Texas she would have to take the Texas bar exam—a frustrating hurdle she resented. In fact, her memory of her life during this period was that she was full of "transition angst." "It was going to be a wonderful chapter, but I couldn't tell yet."

She missed her own family badly. Missing them led her to one of the most important relationships she would ever develop. The rabbi whom Warren replaced, Sidney Wolf, had lived in the community for decades. He had retired a few years earlier, and a number of short-term hires had come and gone before Warren's appointment. Wolf's wife, Bebe, was a sophisticated French woman, whom Elaine had met during the course of Warren's interview.

Bebe Wolf had grown up in Paris and Cincinnati. She was a spit-fire of a woman, and had started the first chapter of Planned Parenthood in Corpus Christi. Given the time and the place, this was an act of considerable courage. Compared to Elaine, she had been much more of a traditional rabbi's wife. For example, she had worked in the community, but not professionally, while being the rabbi's wife. Elaine saw her as a role model. She had mastered the art of raising healthy, stable children in an environment where children are often subjected to the scrutiny and high expectations of the entire community.

> She told me I had to make my friends outside the congregation. This was a small congregation, about one hundred and fifty families. She said in order to have a zone of privacy, you have to have a life outside the congregation. That had been more criti-cal for her than for me, because she didn't work. She intro-duced me to the woman who became my closest friend there. She was wife of the Christian minister and was roughly my own age.
>
> Bebe was my mother's age. I am very close to my mother, but in many ways Bebe slipped into the mother role. She did things for us that my mother would have done for us if she had lived near us. She had us over to Friday night dinner regularly. She

cooked food and brought it over to us. She would bake the children birthday cakes. She had a box of toys in her house that my kids could play with.

There was another thing that Bebe Wolf taught Elaine that Elaine's mother would never have been able to do: she taught her how to figure out the role of rabbi's wife in Corpus Christi, Texas, in a way that worked for her. This was a much more traditional community than the one in California, and now Elaine was the wife of the rabbi himself, not the wife of his assistant. She clearly held a position in the community. She had to find a way to meet her obligations.

She knew right away what she *wouldn't* do—she wouldn't cook. "Never did I play the traditional stand-in-the-kitchen role," she said. "She's not a kitchen girl," her mother agreed years later.

Although she might not have prepared the food for the community Hanukkah party, she attended it, and she went with a sense of her position. She began teaching in the Sunday school—an activity that she soon found she loved. Occasionally she would combine her two lives, by lecturing the adult women on some aspect of Jewish law. She also spent time teaching high school kids. She would have the kids perform plays she had written. Still, even when she was at home full-time, the job of *rebbetzin* was one that Elaine was never interested in exploring to its fullest degree. Or as her mother put it, "She didn't do the rabbi's wife thing."

Her interests lay in the law and in having her own professional identity. There was an economic incentive, too, for going back to work. Both Stones still had loans they had to pay off. Elaine got in touch with a member of the congregation who was a partner in a small local law firm, practicing corporate defense. Elaine was hired, took and passed the local bar exam, joined the firm, and made a close friend all in a matter of weeks.

Then she found out she was pregnant again. Lia Rebecca was born in October 1983. Coming back to work after her second maternity leave, Elaine decided there was no point in working long billable hours at a law firm where she would probably only spend a few years. Why not take the time in Corpus Christi to experiment? She had always been interested in criminal law. Among her new friends she had met and liked was "another transplant," who had a job in the district attorney's office. Elaine decided to move further away from her "normal" career path, applied to work for the DA, and was hired.

To an outsider, such a move seems gutsy and cool. But Elaine saw that by moving to Texas she had stepped off the traditional partnership track for several years and she didn't know if she'd be able to get back on. Which is not to say she regretted it. "Going to a first-rate law firm becomes an option, and there is a momentum. That first law firm in LA was an extraordinary place. I get the announcements whenever they make new partners, and I look at the list and see where my name would fit now if I had stayed there and made partner. I would be way at the top. It's an interesting experience for me whenever that note card comes to show the benefit and the detriment of continuity."

But there was something liberating about the move she had made. She loved her time at the DA's office. Working in criminal law in Corpus Christi gave her a fascinating perspective of the city. She handled the appellate work for the DA, which meant she regularly argued at the appeals court and through this she helped to try a particularly high-profile case. It also meant she reported to the DA himself. The job was what she described as "manageable full-time," and the drive was a few minutes from the house.

By now Nomi was at preschool and the Stones had help. During this period they had a teenage girl who would come in before breakfast and stay through dinner. She took care of the kids and "kept up the house somewhat." In addition, Elaine's mother was a regular visitor.

Meanwhile, Warren was hard at work. He joined several local boards, worked on a number of interfaith projects, and began to raise money to build a new temple. But for him this period was the one when the family could meet for lunch at the local lighthouse, where he could pick the girls up from their preschool (usually the only father in line), and take them on picnics to a special rock behind the art museum. Everything they did was smaller and simpler. This was the time when the family came first.

In late 1985, shortly after Lia had turned two, Elaine got a call from a local attorney, David Perry. Perry was a prominent product liability attorney who was looking for someone to join his firm as an appellate lawyer. Elaine's reputation at the DA's office had begun to spread, and in particular her outstanding writing ability had struck the attention of a local trial judge. She was said to put together briefs that were truly beautiful. Rene Haas, a former prosecutor and the first female elected state district judge in Nueces County, had heard of Elaine. Haas happened to be David Perry's wife. Her instinct told her that hiring Elaine would be the right thing for her husband to do.

Over lunch in his office (not the kind of interview Elaine was used to) Perry asked her if she would be interested in working for him. It was a bolt from the blue. She was happy in her job and had never considered the type of law he was proposing. And yet she had to think about the money. Working for the government had been giving her manageable hours, and she could do it well, but it didn't pay much. This was a chance to have another exciting experience while doing better financially. Working for Perry meant working on a contingency fee, which is when a lawyer takes a percentage of a settlement. She didn't have to show billable hours, she just had to get the work done. That was an attractive prospect. She took the job.

It was much harder work, much longer hours than she had thought. Her memories of Corpus Christi became blurred by exhaustion. She used to drive home and just sit in the car for a few minutes, summoning the energy to go inside to her two little girls, who would cling to her once she walked into the house. Before she got home, the two of them would fight over which of them could get closer to the door and be the first to reach her as she came through. She was working such long hours that she often missed bedtime altogether. But she provided the girls with her presence by recording audiotapes of stories and chats for them to listen to each night—with every tape ending with the instruction to "Brush your teeth!" On the tapes (which the family kept) she made a point of mentioning how much she liked what she was doing and how exciting she found it. She would read books, and chat to the girls, as if she was sitting on their beds. She would punctuate the stories she read with questions about their days. She would wonder what they had had for dinner. The tapes were very soothing. Listening to her chatting away anyone might start to feel relaxed, sleepy and well taken care of.

During those years, her relationship with Bebe grew stronger. Whenever Elaine felt completely exhausted, she would take a two-hour lunch and go to Bebe's house. "She would cook me lunch, give me a pair of her silk pajamas, and I would climb into her water bed and go to sleep. No one would get through—not the office, not Warren, not nobody. It was heaven, absolute heaven. In the last few years I would do that once a month."

Bebe helped in other ways, too. She taught Elaine to protect herself from the demands and the exposure of the Jewish community. There could be so much human need in a community of four hundred to five hundred people. Bebe taught Elaine to create a separate world—a private world—where she could put her needs and the needs of her family first. In that, she had *not* been a traditional rabbi's wife, and she encouraged Elaine to follow her tradition. This was a fairly radical attitude. Both Warren and Elaine had grown up where the rabbi's wife and children were always seated in the front row for services. Largely because of the influence of Bebe and Sidney Wolf, the Stones didn't ask that of their children and took care not to overload them with congregational expectations.

Elaine joined the Perry firm in December 1985, a time of enormous

product liability cases around the country. One of Perry's biggest
case was *Durrill v. Ford Motor Company*,* and Elaine was quickly
drafted to work on the appeal. The case, which ended with a large
award, including punitive damages against Ford, brought Perry national stature, and he was retained in a number of cases all over the
country. Soon Elaine was involved in writing briefs for trials in
Florida, Indiana, and California.

She might have been working much longer hours, but she was
making much more money. She joined the firm as an associate, but
within six months she was on a percentage of the profits of the
firm—Perry had made her a partner. What did this mean? It meant
that in one year she made more money than she would have made
twenty years later as a partner at Covington & Burling. It meant that
she would later have enough of a financial cushion to take five years
off work with no worries. It meant that when the time came to sell
the house in Texas, during the oil slump, the family would be able to
take a loss but still buy a comfortable new home in Bethesda, Maryland. It meant that Warren's rabbinical school loans could get paid
off, and the family would eventually be able to contemplate private
school as an option. Life was hectic but good.

As we have seen throughout this book, marriage is an elastic institution. But the base is important, and the Stones' marriage was based on
a meeting of the minds. Warren might have been a little older and further along the academic path, but he was a progress-minded man in a
progressive time. He respected his future wife's abilities and wanted
her to succeed. They were always proud of each other's achievements,
and from the start each took the other's interests and ambitions
seriously and figured out ways to make their choices coexist.

---

* A rear-end collision fire case in which a 1974 Ford Mustang II exploded into flames. The
two occupants of the vehicle, Devary Durrill and Bonnie Watkins, died of burns. The collision occurred in October 1978, a few months following the famous Pinto recall. The
Mustang II was built from the same vehicle platform as the Pinto and contained the same
defects.

Warren, who conducts a lot of marriage counseling in his role of rabbi, tries to apply what he teaches others to his own marriage. "Marriage is not a contract, it is a covenant," he said. "You have to give more than you receive. You have to give 75 percent, not 50 percent. You have to surprise each other with Zen gifts and moments. You have to get beyond the routine and make each other a priority."

They asked a lot of each other and still do. There has been a lot of compromise in this marriage. Both partners have interrupted their own career for the sake of the other. Both ask each other to carry the load with the children when they need to be at work, or if they just need a break. Each has moved, or delayed moving, because of the other. Neither of them thought that Corpus Christi would be their final destination, but the decision to leave was painful for both of them.

At the outset they agreed to spend roughly three to five years in Corpus Christi. In the end they stayed seven. Warren built the new synagogue; the community thrived under his stewardship; and Elaine, who had found it so hard to settle in, now found the prospect of tearing up the roots she had put down harder still. But there were things they missed. Warren in particular noticed the absence of the cultural life of a larger city. And he was ready to apply what he had done on a micro scale in a small community to a larger one.

When the job of rabbi at Temple Emanuel in Kensington, Maryland, one mile north of the Capital Beltway, opened up, Warren decided to apply for it. The couple felt there was enough in the Washington, D.C., area to make them both happy. In a town full of lawyers there would be plenty of jobs for Elaine to choose from. The Reform community at the new temple was bigger and because of its location could have a more national identity. It was less conservative politically than the Texas community, which made it more of a comfortable fit. D.C. had galleries, museums, and performing arts. And suburban Maryland is a good place to raise kids, with decent public schools and beautiful neighborhoods. Washington had always been a place where the Stones thought they might settle; they had both spent summers there as students. For all of these reasons, it was an attractive choice to several other candidates, too. More than one hundred rabbis were interested in this particular congregation and many were interviewed by the search committee.

When it was his turn to be interviewed, Warren was very clear on two issues: first, his wife would not be part of the rabbinical package; and second, he would need to take one month's sabbatical every year. He had the idea of proposing the regular sabbatical because by the time he left Texas, he was actually due to take a sabbatical, given that he had been in his job for seven years. He liked the idea of having a regular time to explore, develop, and enrich himself, and to devote himself entirely to his family. His thought was that if he could take one month a year, he would spend two weeks of that on some kind of professional development and the other two weeks being a stay-at-home dad and husband. Meanwhile, the community would have a regular opportunity to have other people lead the congregation. Both of Warren's proposals were acceptable to the community, and Warren got the job.

Moving was much more complicated this time. Nomi was now seven, and Lia was five. Warren had to start his job in November right after Thanksgiving. The family decided to finish out the calendar year in Texas and head east in January. Once again Elaine would stop working and get the family settled before picking up again.

In the same way that Warren had hit it off with Sidney Wolf in Texas, he immediately became friendly with the president of the board of the congregation at Temple Emanuel. His new friend was not an older mentor but a contemporary. Mark Mann, the local junior high school principal, was the same age as Warren and also married with young children. Both men were fans of the Grateful Dead. They were the same generation, and they spoke the same language.

The idea of working with someone like that filled Warren with excitement and optimism.

He drove across country with Amber, the family dog, and arrived in Maryland by himself just before Thanksgiving weekend 1988, and Elaine and the girls remained in Texas. Warren was staying at the Manns' house and Mark Mann gave the speech that welcomed Warren to the synagogue that first Friday night. That weekend, in streets still wet from a heavy downpour, Mann's car was hit by a jeep, which skidded through a stop sign. He was killed in the accident.

Warren was devastated. "I went to the hospital and fell apart. And the hospital chaplain said, 'You can't fall apart, you're the rabbi.' I said, 'But I've lost my friend.'" He officiated at the funeral, still reeling from the shock.

I couldn't imagine what it must have been like for him to have had to go through this alone, with his family so far away. I was surprised that his wife hadn't flown east to be with him, as he had to cope with being the new rabbi in such traumatic circumstances. But he saw it differently. First, he and Elaine had decided she should stay with the girls: they were in their own upheaval over the impending move. He joked that he was glad he had brought his dog with him. Then he grew more serious. "You walk through the grief with the people that you serve," he said. "With the shatteredness came a closeness to a community that might have taken a few years to develop."

He didn't have his wife beside him during those terrible weeks, but he did have his religion and his community. Warren received tremendous emotional sustenance from those he served, and he recognized his own need to be alone after periods of intense service. This was why he had stipulated he should get the month's sabbatical each year as he came into Temple Emanuel.

He is still the rabbi there almost twenty years later, and he still takes his sabbaticals. Over the years he has spent his time away in a variety of places, with Jewish communities in Spain or Turkey, at the

Jung Institute in Switzerland, hiking through Vermont, on rabbinical trips through Jordan and Israel with colleagues, on retreat at Esalen near San Francisco.

He plays a vital role not just in the family but also in the house. But for the weeks when he's gone, Elaine has to adjust, be a single parent, and carry the entire load. But Warren is the type of husband who really pulls his weight. He has often been home when Elaine was at work; he cooks, he drives, and he likes to buy things for the house.

Moving to Maryland with two young girls was a different prospect from moving with one small baby. To make it as painless for Nomi and Lia as she could, Elaine wanted to get the move over with as quickly as possible. She didn't want to rent a house while looking for a place to buy. She wanted to move only once. "We moved right into the house we are in now. We went back and forth and bought it on a weekend. It was brand-new, not even completely built yet when we saw it. It made me nuts having to do everything so quickly, but we were trying to minimize the trauma of moving by not moving into a rental and then again, but just doing it all at once."

The house was finished by the time they arrived, and Elaine worked to get the kids settled at school. Again in an attempt to ease the move, she decided to put the girls into the local elementary school together, even though Lia was only just five and had been in pre-school in Texas. She thought it would be easier for Lia to change schools just once, even though her decision meant Lia would be young for her class for the rest of her academic career.

Despite Elaine's efforts, the move was tough, especially for Nomi. Arriving in the middle of a school year, with a Texan accent, having left her best friend behind, knowing no one, was excruciating. Years later Nomi spoke of how hard she found it. "I was eight years old, in second grade. It was a very rocky adjustment. I was very shy. We came halfway through the year. That first year was horrible. She didn't work for the first few months and every day she would come to pick me up from school twenty minutes early. She would do this little shivery dance outside the window that I could see. It was so reassuring. I was so distraught at school."

Of course, Elaine had to look around for a new job again. But then something seemed to fall right into her lap. A friend she had clerked with in Maine knew of a job on Capitol Hill, working on the impeachment of judge Alcee Hastings. The Senate legal counsel, Mike Davidson, got Elaine's name from her former colleague and her résumé. By now it boasted an eye-catching combination of experience. He liked what he saw. He was impressed with her judicial clerkship, and that she had worked in a prosecutor's office and knew criminal law. When Davidson met Elaine, he noticed that not only was she very bright, but she was also "extraordinarily fair, which I thought was indispensable."

Davidson recommended her to senators Jeff Bingaman and Arlen Specter, who were co-chairs of the impeachment committee, and in March 1989 she began work. The whole process took seven months. To sum up what was a complicated process, the House had voted to try Judge Hastings on seventeen acts of misconduct, including conspiring to obtain a $150,000 bribe while he was a federal judge in Florida. The Senate committee's role was to conduct the trial with the House acting as Hastings's prosecutor. The Senate had already agreed that the impeachment committee would hear and receive evidence in the case, and would then provide the full Senate with a written summary of what they had learned in a way that would both fairly provide each side's position and help the Senate understand how those positions coincided and differed. Elaine served as counsel to the committee. As Davidson described it, it was Elaine who was responsible for the document that the full Senate eventually received for deliberation. It was her concept, her execution, and her imprint.

On October 20, 1989, the U.S. Senate found Hastings guilty on eight impeachable counts, including accepting the $150,000 bribe, and removed him from office.* After a few more weeks of tying up loose ends, Elaine's work was done. It had been a brief but intense period of work, but it was to have enormous consequences on her future.

Meanwhile, she had another job offer. David Perry hadn't wanted to lose Elaine and he had a case back in Austin which needed her help. The case involved a woman who had been seriously injured when the ATV she was riding in rolled over. It was due to go to trial in early 1990 and Perry asked Elaine to return to Austin to try the case with him. Elaine agreed, thinking the trial would last a few weeks. In fact it lasted six months—far longer than she had anticipated. This was a time of extraordinary strain for the family. Every week she flew back and forth to Austin, leaving Bethesda on Sunday evening and returning on Thursday night. "It was brutal!" she remembered.

Before she left she would lay out the girls clothes to wear each day while she was gone. "The period when she was going back and forth to Texas—it was horrible. I remember having fights with my sister and calling her to solve it because she was my mom. My dad couldn't solve it," said Lia, her voice rising and sounding years younger as she talked about this period. Lia's memory made the time seem traumatic. "She was doing her best. She was present even when she wasn't. She was always very involved. But when she was missing everything would fall apart. Who would do my hair? Who would do my ponytail in the morning for school?"

Warren, with the housekeeper, did his best to hold things to-gether in his wife's absence, but with limited appreciation from his

---

* In September 1992, Federal District Judge Stanley Sporkin found the Senate's use of the trial committee to be improper, and essentially reversed Hastings's Senate conviction, but the Supreme Court then ruled in a similar case that the courts could not review Senate impeachment proceedings. So the Senate's verdict and Hastings's removal from office stood. The Senate had had the option of forbidding Hastings to hold Federal office again but had chosen not to exercise the option. While challenging the Senate's verdict in the courts, Hastings had been running for Congress. Two months after Sporkin's ruling, Hastings was elected to the House of Representatives which had voted to impeach him in the first place.

daughters. "He couldn't be the mom," said Nomi. "He didn't have the skills."

We've seen a number of husbands who commute long distances for extended periods of time in this book. We've learned about Sherry Goff who took a lengthy sabbatical from her family while on an internship. Now there's Elaine Stone, a wife, who—like Keith Coleman and Warren Feder—had to spend a large part of each week working far from her daughters. As with Sherry, the absence of the mother seemed to take a far bigger toll on the children than the absence of the father. For it was clear that as much as Warren tried to fill in the blanks, the girls needed Elaine and she knew it and felt torn. She couldn't just leave the house on Sunday, she had leave a part of herself behind. That was the reason behind all the elaborate preparations. She had to be present even when she wasn't. But when she was in Texas she could concentrate solely on working, and she wanted the girls to know how important her work was to her.

Once the trial was won in August 1990, Perry asked Elaine to continue to work for him from Maryland. She came home for the rest of the summer and arranged to set up an office in her home and telecommute to Texas. In the short term this seemed like a good move. Her former secretary flew in to help her convert the basement of the new house. The room was lined with volumes of law books, but in those days there was no Internet or e-mail. Telecommuting wasn't as efficient or as common as it is now. There was just a phone, a fax, and lots of files. Occasionally she had to fly back to Texas for meetings but other than than she remained at home, with her head in the basement office but much more available. "I was very hungry to be around, to be at home [after the trial]," she said.

The problem with telecommuting is it can be both isolating and never-ending. "I could hear the fax machine ringing all the time," said Elaine. "I did get the work done, but a great deal of my pleasure and fun is the people with whom I work and exchange ideas. Telecommuting took away that piece of it."

Warren and Elaine had originally planned to have three children, but their jobs and moves had postponed any thought of a third child until now. Elaine was thirty-nine years old, they were settled in Bethesda, and things were fairly calm. If they were going to have that third child, this would be the time to do it.

Elaine became pregnant in late 1991. Her late pregnancy mirrored her own mother's experience, and the two girls were as ecstatic at the prospect of a new baby as Elaine's brothers had been with her. This pregnancy was very much a communal experience from the time Warren and Elaine brought the early sonogram pictures to dinner. Nomi, who was in sixth grade, read *What to Expect When You're Expecting* from cover to cover. Both girls felt maternal and protective from the start.

Zachary Stone was born in August 1992. The Stone family's gain was David Perry's loss. "We tried to make the telecommuting thing work," he said resignedly years later. "But when Zach was born, I think it was just too much of a strain, and I think she recognized that she wanted to spend more time with the family than would really work out." Within months of Zach's birth, Elaine had quit. "It was a gift I gave myself and my family."

She came up from the basement and stayed in the house. "Finally my heart was upstairs, not downstairs," she said. Why did she quit the workforce *now*? Was it because she felt confident enough to leave a strong career, knowing she could, and would resume it when the time was right? Was it because she loved her new and final baby? Was it because she had two school-age girls she needed to spend more time with? Was she tired of being pulled in so many directions? Did she see that life as a stay-at-home mom in Washington, D.C., wouldn't be boring or isolating? Or was the decision a financial one? She could do this now because she could finally afford to. She had earned it.

For all of those reasons Elaine stayed home, and every member of the Stone family recalled this as a magical time of their lives. Warren remembered it as the golden time of his marriage, the girls think of it as the best years of their childhood, Elaine describes it as the "glorious stretch" of her family life, and Zach—Zach was too young to know any better. They didn't have to worry about money; they didn't have to worry about time. They didn't have to worry about the future; they had made a plan. Elaine would stay at home for five years. After that she would look for work. She was confident she would find it. She always had.

What was it like suddenly being a stay-at-home mother? She had been a professional woman for so long. Part of the appeal for Elaine was the intense bond she felt with Zachary. But she also loved getting reconnected with Warren and reinvolved in his life. His working hours (he was busiest during the evenings and on weekends) meant he had been able to do his share with the kids when she was working and vice versa. But running a family as a relay race means the husband and wife only get to see each other on the run. For too long Warren and Elaine's interaction had been in snatched moments when one was coming in the door and the other was leaving. Now they could do things together. Warren's day off was Monday. The couple planned their Mondays joyfully. They would drop the girls off at school and then go out to breakfast. They would go to museums, galleries, and bookstores. They developed favorite places and revisited them.

Elaine began to play a much more visible role in the temple, too. She stepped up her role as a rabbi's wife. "With a friend, I wrote a theatrical piece about the Holocaust, which she then directed. The focus was on 'rescuers,' people who stepped forward at enormous risk to save others. It was a big production at the temple and involved, mostly adults, a few children. My motivation was wanting to find a way to introduce the subject to children in a way that did not utterly defeat hope, but its audience was adults as well as kids."

The girls, who were now headed to middle school, also benefited enormously. Their mother would pick them up from school, and she would be there to help with homework—she even cooked. She bought *The Moosewood Cookbook,* composed of simple vegetarian recipes and for the first time, took over this part of family life. When Nomi got into a creative writing middle school in Silver Spring, half an hour's drive away, the distance wasn't a problem. Elaine picked her up every day with Zachary in a car seat in the back. "She was so there; she wanted to know every inch of my day. She was in the car when I came out upset because I didn't get a role in the play."

Elaine was 100 percent at home. She didn't go to networking lunches; she didn't attend seminars. She read the paper, she read books, and she thought of writing one, too, of all the children's stories she had made up and taped while she was commuting. She went to the gym a lot, took care of her kids, cooked, and paid attention to her husband. She was happy. But she knew this was a finite thing. She had a five-year plan, and she knew that once those five years were up, things would change.

I asked her once if she ever felt a lack of self-confidence as the years passed, if she had nervousness that when her time at home was up she might not find it easy to reenter the workforce. Of course she was nervous, she replied. She sometimes wondered what she would do next, and how easy it was going to be to find the "next." But she didn't dwell on it. For five years her focus was to be on her home.

Zachary started Georgetown Day School in September 1998. He was now a kindergartner and gone for the school day. Nomi was seventeen and Lia fifteen. They were independent high school girls with their thoughts on boys and college. There was an obvious decline in the family's need for Elaine, and she began to think about how she should return to work.

When your law firm becomes your peer group and your colleagues describe themselves as your family, you don't need to work at staying in touch; your relationships are solid friendships and endure over the years. Just as David Perry hadn't wanted to lose Elaine, Mike Davidson had kept in touch with her during her time at home and had periodically called her to offer her more work. Previously she had said no, but suddenly his timing was perfect.

In the late fall of 1998, exactly when Elaine was looking for something to do, Davidson called with an offer. Like the Hastings trial, this was a specific short-term project. Davidson had been asked by a coalition of two Washington think tanks, the American Enterprise Institute and the Brookings Institution, to evaluate the independent counsel statute that was about to expire. The independent counsel law had to be renewed by Congress every five years. Controversy about the law was at its height because of President Clinton and independent counsel Kenneth Starr.* There were questions about whether the law should be renewed at all. Should it be changed? If so, what should those changes be?

The panel that convened to examine its future was a roster of heavy-hitting names, including the one-time attorney general nominee Judge Zoë Baird, the future Supreme Court chief justice John Roberts, former attorney general Dick Thornburgh, U.S. trade representative Carla Hills, representatives Bill Paxton and David Skaggs, and former solicitor general Drew Days. They all met regularly under the co-chairmanship of senators Bob Dole and George Mitchell. Mike Davidson was the counsel, and Elaine would be the associate counsel. As before, their roles would be to compile the material, advise the group as it reached its conclusions and recommendations, and make sense of it all in a final document.

"This was a group that was more than decorative; they were seriously engaged," remembered Davidson. "They had confidence in delegating, but they were not going to sign off on something they did not believe in." For Elaine, this was a perfect reentry. It was fascinating work with first-rate people. It would have a definite impact,

---

* President Bill Clinton appointed Kenneth Starr to the Office of the Independent Counsel to investigate the death of the deputy White House counsel Vince Foster and the Whitewater land transactions. He later submitted to Congress the Starr Report, which led to Clinton's impeachment on charges arising from the Monica Lewinsky scandal.

and the hours were manageable. The panel published its report in May 1999. Davidson stayed on for a few weeks to help prepare some of the members testify before Congress, and Elaine went home.

Zachary was in a class at school with a little boy named Sam Breuer whose father, Lanny, was special counsel to president Bill Clinton. This was the time when people at school kept getting the two families mixed up. Teachers were getting the mothers confused. Parents would go up to Nancy Breuer and ask how her husband the rabbi was. Naturally this led to the families talking to each other more than they might have done, and Lanny in particular became intrigued with Elaine's background. Elaine saw where this could lead.

> Before [the Brookings project] ended, I was thinking about what would be next. It seemed time to me to move into work that would have a life beyond the duration of a specific project. I was already talking to Lanny as a result of the connection at school. Warren, Nancy, Lanny, and I had become friends. I remember one particular evening when the four of us went out, when we ended up talking in some detail about the various things I had done. The impeachment, in particular, came up.

Breuer thought Elaine could be very useful to him and his team. "In 1998 Lewinsky hit," he said.

> I was put on the investigations team reporting to White House Counsel Chuck [Charles] Ruff. I was told to think through what an impeachment trial would look like. I had known that Elaine had done a couple of impeachment hearings, and I was beginning to ask her what she thought. I asked her to come to the White House and talk to Chuck Ruff and me and maybe a third colleague. She was spectacular. Thoughtful, well reasoned, and well prepared. It would be an exaggeration to say

she provided the blueprint of what we did, but she helped me think what an impeachment would look like.

Clinton was impeached by the House of Representatives on December 19, 1988, and acquitted by the Senate the following February while Elaine was still working at Brookings. Breuer hadn't forgotten how impressive she had been, and he knew when the Brookings project ended she would be looking for work. At Covington & Burling, from which he had taken a leave to work for Clinton, he co-chaired the white-collar practice, and in 1999, when he returned to the law firm from the White House, as he put it, "I had my eyes set on Elaine. . . What I knew was that if you had someone really smart and really nice, you could make it work. I *knew* that once she was in the door everyone would love her. I was really frantic that we had to make her an offer, so I romanced her in a work sense."

Breuer had to convince his fellow partners that hiring Elaine made sense. He got them to take a close look at her résumé, and they liked what they saw. They liked that she had been at Munger, Tolles in California, a law firm they considered a peer. And they thought "the funky stuff," as they put it, gave her perspective. She had been a plaintiff's lawyer and a prosecutor. Her idiosyncratic experience gave her a range.

Elaine joined the firm in November 1999 and from the start was a hit. She was extremely confident. She quickly identified partners she wanted to work with and approached them. Professionally she came across as assured and capable.

Partners at Covington describe a professional environment that to an outsider sounds deceptively informal. They talk about "sticking your head in" to someone's office, of doors that are always open to those who want to offer to help. That might be. Or it may be so to an older, more experienced, more confident hire. It's hard to imagine everyone feeling capable of walking into the office of a senior partner with an almighty reputation, offering to help and walking out with a bunch of briefs.

Bruce Baird, a senior partner at the law firm, who had previously been an assistant U.S. attorney in Manhattan, told me, "It quickly became clear that she could work very well and analyze very well. She was a perfectionist. She sweats the details. Her standards were really high. I would really lean on her. She could keep all the details in place. She can take on a case. Given a legal situation, she can understand the pieces and is a real self-starter."

But it wasn't quite that utopian. Elaine's real skill lay in hiding her own struggles. In fact, her first day back at work was tough. Her first assignment was to represent the Exxon Pipeline Company, in a Freedom of Information Act dispute. "It was a hard, sudden immersion. I had not done civil litigation of this nature in quite some time; I hadn't practiced law at all in more than five years."

While she had been away, technology had revolutionized the workplace. There were computers to master and research to be conducted online. The methods for court filings had changed. If she had a problem, though, she didn't show it. She took what she was given to do, figured out how to do it, and moved on. Because of this she was promoted extraordinarily quickly. After one year she was made "of counsel," and in 2004 she became partner. Nationally, in 2004 women made up only 17.1 percent of partners in law firms. Obviously Elaine was more than capable at her job, but she was also very clear about what it was that she wanted. "She would sit down on my couch and say, 'I want to be a partner,' " said Breuer. "We would plan her path. I and others pushed her quickly. She has a quiet confidence; she can stand up for herself. In her own charming way she lets you know she wants it. She is not obnoxious. I thought that if she didn't make partner, I would feel guilty every single day. I have enough to feel guilty about. I didn't want to be guilt ridden. And I didn't want to lose her. I wanted to do right by her."

Not everyone in the firm was immediately convinced as Breuer and Baird were. Some partners wondered whether she was getting a partnership too quickly; others asked whether she was enough of a leader. But they were outnumbered and eventually proved wrong. After she became partner, she informally mentored several associates at the firm, joined the partnership's work-life committee, juggled cases, and positioned herself to play a leadership role in the firm. She was asked to take on one of the firm's key roles, as a managing partner with responsibility for 210 associates in the Washington, D.C., office. If that role contained maternal elements, it reflected professional choices she continued to make. She was, after all, a mother. She preferred to manage cases, not find them. She strategized on big matters, coordinated all the moving pieces, delegated work to more junior members of a team, and, as always, continued to write or edit material. She was one of 36 women partners at the firm, representing about 20 percent of the 175 partnership total. Covington had elected its first woman partner in 1974, just when Elaine was looking at law schools. By 2005 roughly 30 percent of the firm's lawyers were women. Although a new partner, Elaine was one of the more senior in terms of years in practice. As such, she had felt a responsibility to the women below her. Yet she still had several years of her own career ahead of her. She regularly discussed her future with Breuer and Baird.

Baird believed she had the potential to become a rainmaker and bring big clients into the firm. Breuer, who got to know her as a mother first, saw her as having an important part to play within the firm, possibly as a member of the management committee someday. He thought that both the example of her own life story and the interest she took in the younger members of the firm would serve her well in that regard.

Meanwhile, as she continued to juggle work and family, life went on at home. Her mother died in 2006—a huge blow to Elaine, who had been forced to delay a number of trips to visit her due to pressures of work. Nomi and Lia finished college and found pre-graduate school work in D.C.; Zachary began high school. Warren continued to run the temple, take his sabbatical, and cook the evening meal. He was becoming increasingly active in the world beyond his own community, growing into a national figure speaking out on religion and the environment.

Of the three children, only Zachary was interested in the law. He loved talking about his mother's cases with her on the way home from school in the car, he told me. He admired her career and thought about becoming a lawyer himself one day, too.

The family continued to come together to heap adoration on Zachary, their baby. In 2006 they all went on a family vacation to Spain. Zach, who had spent the first five years of his life as the undiluted object of everyone's attention, was growing up with the confidence of knowing he was the center of the Stone family universe. At one dinner in Spain he sat listening to his iPod while his parents and two sisters gazed at him lovingly. When he looked up and noticed the collective interest, he grinned and had one thing to say, which is a fitting last word from the child of this chapter.

"Get your own life."

Epilogue

JUST BEFORE I finished writing this book, I ducked out of town for three days to go on a mini-vacation with forty-eight other middle-age mothers. Some in our group had never stopped working, some had, and some had completely reinvented themselves. There were entrepreneurs and divorcées, happy and unhappy wives. In short, it was the smorgasbord of experience and the diversity of background one expects from any get-together of this size at this juncture of life.

Yet I was more struck by our similarities than our differences. At dinner on our first night in Montana we counted up the collective number of children we had left behind (nobody thought to count the husbands or partners). When we got to our grand total of ninety, a spontaneous cheer erupted around the room. That cheer gave me the feeling that we were all in this together. And we are.

I don't know whether or not you believe in the competition between working and stay-at-home mothers. I don't know if you are "for" any particular choices a mother makes and "against" others. I choose not to play that game. And I don't believe we should indulge it. Ask any woman which relationships matter to her most in the world, and near the top of the list you will find "girlfriends." We are all on the same team.

This book has celebrated the times women have worked and the times they have been at home. It has explored one way of doing both, which is to do them serially. This might end up being your way, or it might not. Whatever you end up choosing, don't judge yourself—enjoy yourself.

Over the last few years, I have often been asked to generalize about women's experiences in balancing work and family. Generally, I have found those experiences (not just the ones in the book) to be positive. Things don't seem to be too bad. Is it a coincidence that my strongest impression happens to be my most positive impression? I've observed an encouraging shift in focus as women begin to adjust to a life of motherhood. At some point we think less of "having" and more about "giving." It's the "doing" that we have to figure out. As mothers we want to live lives of meaning. We think about the example we are setting for our children and the legacy we will leave them. To put it in a Hallmark vernacular, we want to make their world a better place.

Those of us who stay at home start giving on a small scale by taking care of our babies and running our households. Those who go back to work often start thinking about mentoring, as Elaine Stone did. Stay-at-home mothers who are thinking about going back to work are often drawn to volunteer work, not just because it is easy to get and builds confidence but because it feels good. We want to make a difference, whether it's on a micro scale like Sherry Goff, or a larger one like Lauren Jacobson.

We all network—it's in our natures—but we're not crazy about the word. It doesn't reflect the organic way we chat and pass on names, tips, and ideas without thinking. We like to put people together, and our business associates often become our friends. We like to like the people we work with.

We also like to join things. This can be an invaluable and easy asset if we are trying to rejoin the workforce. We like organizations—not just the ones that recruit former housewives back into business, but all of them. Just as we have been identified as being brand loyal in what we buy, we are loyal to the places we join. Whether it's a book club, gym, church, charity, school, or professional organization— even a Web site—we network there. And we are good at it. If you don't know how to begin to get back to work, start at these places, where your friends are. You won't feel intimidated, and you'll be amazed at the help and advice you receive.

I found all the women in this book by asking. It was the only thing I could think of to do. I had nothing to lose. There was nothing at stake at the beginning; I just had an idea. I asked my friends. I asked the parents waiting outside the classrooms at school. I asked people I used to work with and people I worked out with. I called everyone I knew and everyone I used to know, particularly those who had moved away to other parts of the world. It was like dropping a stone into a pond. The people I asked, asked the people they knew and on and on. I could have been asking for any kind of information, so you can, too. If you are feeling overwhelmed and intimidated at the prospect of either quitting or going back to work and you don't know how to do it, just ask. You'll get the help you need.

Whether she's a doctor or a lawyer, a mother's primary focus will always be her children. You know this if you are a mother yourself. No matter what we do, or where we are, we constantly talk about our kids. We talk much, much less about our husbands or partners. I first noticed this when I was interviewing the women whose stories you've just read. They would chat away for hours about their off-spring, remembering tiny details of what they did as babies, and barely mention their husbands. It's as if our children are an integral part of our identities—if I am telling you about my daughter's eye-sight, or my son's soccer, I am telling you something about myself. Where does that leave our husbands? Milling about on the sidelines?

Over time and with children, the role a husband plays in our life changes. Marriage vows are expected to be rigid, though a high divorce rate makes us wonder how rigid. The reality is that marriages are fluid. Your partner might be a central figure, the primary breadwinner, a supporting cast member, a friend and cheerleader, an adversary, a business partner, or all of the above. He might be absent or present. He has his own needs and his own life. Once upon a time, he got married, made a home, and left his family in it. These days he gets married and has no idea where he is headed. He might pay for the house; he might stay home and clean it. His marriage might be a constant or it might be constantly reinvented. Today's husband has become less proactive and more reactive, which is a good thing—if he knows what he is meant to be reacting to. You'll notice that the happiest marriages in this book, those that most successfully weathered the changes, were the ones with a give-and-take. This might sound like obvious advice, but if you want your partner to feel involved in your life, you need to involve him.

Reinventing a marriage and combining work and family in a serial way is widely appealing because we love to change ourselves. Even if we are passionate about what we do, or what we did, we are constantly changing and we like to change our landscapes accordingly. Did you ever think when you left college that you would work at the same place for the rest of your life? Did you really believe your first job would be your last? Are you the same person now as you were then? Don't you celebrate the differences? Okay, maybe not the physical differences, but you know what I mean.

You might have noticed that each of these chapters has ended with the women looking toward their futures. As I said at the start, it's logical to think of a comeback as a move forward. This is why the first job back isn't necessarily the last one. Yes, Sherry is still happily ensconced in her school district, but Elaine, Lauren, and Judith are more typical. It's not just that their professional needs changed; their family circumstances did, too, and they looked to alter their jobs accordingly.

An adaptability to the movement and changes of life makes us well suited to project-based work. You work on something, you give it your all, it's over. You leave it behind. Remember Ellen Warner saying, "Been there, done that" about her photography? At the time, she said it with satisfaction, not nostalgia, and then when it suited her, she came back to it again. Projects can be well suited to flow with the demands of our families. Sometimes you're around a lot, sometimes not. Remember that line your child learns in preschool, "Mommy always comes back"? She does. As this book shows, in more than one way! And if she has accomplished something she's proud of while she's been gone, she comes back in a good mood.

To some extent all work is project-based. Elaine Stone goes from case to case. Peg French and Sherry Goff from patient to patient or from client to client. Maxine's furniture pieces are each individual projects, as are Ellen's photo shoots. Each deal that Judith works on is its own project. Gearing up for and winding down from projects gives life a natural rhythm, in the same way that dividing a life into sections does. If you think of your life in terms of that rhythm, you might find the prospect of returning to work less daunting. If you think about finding a project to work on rather than a job, you might be less intimidated by the search. It's a question of semantics anyway—whether project or job, we're still talking about work.

Many women I have spoken to recognize that they would love a project they could dive into intensely for a few weeks or months, after which they would return to full-time status at home for a while. The "new" part-time could be defined in terms of dividing a year, not a week. If that's the case, then you could be looking at comeback after comeback in one lifetime. Look at Lauren Jacobson's life. She quit. She went back to work. She quit again. And now she's back.

The other day I received a flyer in the mail advertising a new Little Gym for kids. "Daily allowance of self-esteem" ran the headline on the front. Inside, an enormous font shouted "35 pounds of raw confidence." The Little Gym says, "The greatest gift we can give our children is confidence." What a great marketing ploy. We can buy confidence and "give" it to our kids. Garrison Keillor and his crew up at Lake Wobegon were onto something when they invented Powder Milk Biscuits made from whole wheat that "give shy persons the strength to get up and do what needs to be done." If only. Life might be a lot easier if we could buy our confidence like so much hamburger meat or powdered milk biscuits.

We all feel insecure, shy, and anxious. Look at what some of the mothers did for their daughters in this book, and you'll notice how hard they worked to instill confidence in them. They know what a valuable quality it is, perhaps because they had periods without it themselves. Look at Elaine's childhood drama lessons and Maxine's art courses. Look at Ellen, who had precious little encouragement from her own mother, cheering on her own artistic daughter.

The greatest hurdle you have to overcome in returning to work is the one inside your own head. Think of imposing your will on the world. If you don't think you can find work or sell yourself, you won't. All the women in this book suffered from crises of confidence, and all of them struggled through. It would be nice to be more gung-ho and say they "powered through" those times. But you know they didn't. They struggled. They were just like you. But look at what they accomplished while they were at home. Look at Judith's twins or Lauren's boys. Look at the moves across states and countries. Think about Elaine setting up house in Corpus Christi, alone and boiling hot. These stories don't appear on their résumés, but they have been included in this book because they are part of who these women are. A life is more than a career.

The week I returned home from Montana, a couple of news stories had everyone talking. The first was "new" research that showed women were now less happy than ever. Oh, great! Not only are adult women less happy than adult men, but high school girls are now less happy than their male counterparts. Apparently the problem is that we have too much choice, and it's making us miserable.

What are we supposed to do with this information? Feel better that we feel worse? I felt exasperated. All choice involves sacrifice. If you choose one path over another, then put your energy into the path you're on, not on the one you left behind. Here's some more obvious advice: there will always be studies and reports like these. Ignore the ones that bring you down.

The same week that this unhappy new research was published, the Iranian president came to New York to give a speech at Columbia University. His speech took place at the top of the street of my daughters' school. As I arrived to pick up Molly, I found barricades and police everywhere, sirens blaring and helicopters circling overhead. I immediately felt the same sense of excitement I remembered from the action stories of my youth. Molly felt it, too. As she came to the door of the school building, she thrust her backpack at me. "Come on!" she shouted with an energy I no longer possess. "I have to go and look!" And she ran—tomorrow's girl—past the barricades, up to the top of the hill, to see for herself what all the fuss was about.

Acknowledgments

I am married to a great editor—Bill Keller. He did not edit this book but he has given my life a shape and meaning that informs its pages. The optimism I have expressed in writing comes directly from my happiness with him, as his wife and as the mother of our two daughters. I'd like to thank him for "it all."

I owe so much to the ensemble cast of seven stars: Judith, Maxine, Sherry, Peg, Ellen, Lauren, and Elaine. I'd like to thank them for their time and trust, for their insights and honesty. This book ended up being more of a collaboration than any piece of work I have ever done and I've loved that about it.

I'd also like to thank the supporting players of husbands, children, parents, friends, and coworkers for their time. In particular, thanks to Warren, Larry, Barclay, Miner, Keith, and Warren.

And thanks to readers, mothers, and hardworking women everywhere. The story continues online courtesy of Kimberly Brooks and Jessica Robins-Thompson at Lightray. Thanks to them we have an amazing Web site where you can post your story, ask or give advice, and even arrange a virtual visit with your book group. Log on to www.thecomebackbook.com for more information.

Thanks to Suzanne Gluck at William Morris—agent and friend. Karen Rinaldi bought the book for Bloomsbury and Gillian Blake edited it—thanks to them. Also thanks to Colin Dickerman, Liz

Peters, Maya Baran, and Yelena Gitlin for publishing and publicizing it.

Thank you Anna Bengel and Matt Hermann for research help.

And thanks to Jill Abramson, Charlotte Bauer, Lisa Belkin, Tricia Brock, Frank Bruni, Brigitte Chauvigne, Melanie Cook, Margie Fox, Muriel Gonzalez, Gail Gregg, Emma Hanbury, Angela Janklow, Bob Kerrey, Katie Killean, Michael Kimmelman, Sheryl Longin, Gerry Marzorati, Stacy Mason, Kathleen McCarty, Deborah Needleman, Sarah Paley, Graciela Pena, Frank Rich, Joanne Sellar, Jeannine Shao Collins, Michael Shapiro, Risa Shapiro, Rona Silverton, John and Dana Tierney, Suzanne Todd, and Paula and Fareed Zakaria.

This book began with a dedication to Molly and Alice. Thanks to them for being greater than the sum of their parents. My mother died in 1983, so she never got to see me live this life. Bill's mother died last year while I was in the middle of writing and I miss the conversations we used to have about raising a family. I'd like to end by thanking our fathers, George Keller and Anthony Gilbey, who love and support us in all that we do.

Notes

Introduction

1. Peggy Orenstein, *Flux: Women on Sex, Work, Love, Kids, and Life in a Half-Changed World* (New York: Anchor Books, 2001).

2. Caroline Bird, *Everything a Woman Needs to Know to Get Paid What She's Worth* (New York: McKay, 1973) and *Everything a Woman Needs to Know to Get Paid What She's Worth . . . in the 1980s* (New York: Bantam, 1981).

3. Arlie Hochschild, *The Second Shift* (New York: Penguin, 2003).

4. Sylvia Ann Hewlett and Carolyn Buck Luce, "Extreme Jobs: The Dangerous Allure of the 70-Hour Workweek," *Harvard Business Review* 84, no. 12 (December 2006): 49–59.

5. "National Compensation Survey: Employee Benefits in Private Industry in the United States" (Washington, D.C.: Bureau of Labor Statistics, March 2006).

Judith Feder

1. Tom and Sara Pendergast, eds., "The 1980s: The Way We Lived," in *Bowling, Beatniks, and Bell Bottoms,* vol. 5 (Detroit: U•X•L./Thomson Gale, 2002).

2. Greenspan was so sure of his diagnosis that Warren had a bet with him about it. The two men bet ten thousand dollars, and Warren paid the money in 2002.

3. "Sick children fare better when their parents are present to provide health care. Whether the child's illness be chronic or acute and whether the treatment be at home or in the hospital, parental involvement helps children heal better and faster." Harvard School of Public Health, "Paid Leave Best Predictor of Parents' Ability to Care for Sick Children," press release, August 12, 1999.

4. Jeff Meshel, *One Phone Call Away: Secrets of a Master Networker* (New York: Portfolio, 2005).

5. Anne Marie Chaker and Hilary Stout, "Mothers Who Take Time Off Must Play Career Catch-Up," *Wall Street Journal* Online, May 18, 2004. Available at http://careerpath.org/myc/workfamily/20040518-chaker.html.

Maxine Snider

1. In *A History of Women in the United States: Historical Articles on Women's Lives and Activities,* ed.Nancy F. Cott (New York: K. G. Saur, 1992), this period is described as being a time when housewives were sent a number of conflicting messages about their roles. On the one hand they were encouraged by magazines to leave the house and help in the war effort by working, yet at the same time government officials like Nancy Brown, the Detroit New Women's Advisor, told women in 1940 that as long as their "children were still of school age . . . they do need you. It would not be possible for you to carry on two jobs, one outside your home and one inside" (Cott 371). A good patriot should be a good mother.

2. Beverly Russell, *Women of Design: Contemporary American Interiors* (New York: Rizzoli, 1992).

Sherry Goff

1. Abby Ellin, "As Older Students Return to Classrooms an Industry Develops, *New York Times,* November 11, 2006.

2. Albert R. Karr, " 'Boot Camps' Retrain Mid-life Job Hoppers," *Wall Street Journal* Online, July 12, 2000. Available at http://careerpath.org/jobhunting/change/20000731-karr.html.

3. Peg Tyre, "Learning to Adapt: Community Colleges Offer Older Workers an Affordable Way to Reinvent Themselves and Find Their Place in a Changing Economy," *Newsweek,* June 19, 2006.

4. David D. Corbett, *Portfolio Life: The New Path to Work, Purpose, and Passion After 50* (San Francisco: Jossey-Bass, 2007).

5. Stephen M. Pollan and Mark Levine, *Second Acts: Creating the Life You Really Want, Building the Career You Truly Desire* (New York: HarperResource, 2003).

Ellen Warner

1. Naomi Rosenblum, *A History of Women Photographers* (New York: Abbeville Press, 1994).

2. Obituary by E. M. Morgan, "Joseph Warren: A Gentleman Departs," *Harvard Law Review* 56, no. 2 (October 1942): 171–72.

3. George E. Vaillant, *Aging Well: Surprising Guideposts to a Happier Life from the Landmark Harvard Study of Adult Development* (Boston: Little, Brown, 2002): 47.

Peg French

1. Mary Lou Schmidt, associate professor of pediatrics, University of Illinois College of Medicine. "Finding the Balance Point Between Overdrive and the Mommy Track," in *This Side of Doctoring: Reflections from Women in Medicine*, ed., Eliza Lo Chin (Thousand Oaks, CA: Sage Publications, 2001): 206.

2. R. Henryk-Gutt and R. Silverstone, "Career Problems of Women Doctors," *British Medical Journal* 2, no. 6035 (September 4, 1976): 574–77.

3. Joan Casell, *The Woman in the Surgeon's Body* (Cambridge, MA: Harvard University Press, 1998): 23.

4. Robert Wood Johnson Foundation, "Time Pressures Leave Doctors Dissatisfied" (July 2002), report available at http://www.rwjf.org/reports/grr/027069 .htm.

5. Marjorie A. Bowman et al., *Women in Medicine: Career and Life Management* (New York: Springer, 2002).

6. V. L. Katz, N. H. Miller, and W. A. Bowes Jr., "Pregnancy Complications of Physicians," *Western Journal of Medicine* 149, no. 6 (December 1998): 704–707.

7. Liza Sharpless Bonanno, "Body Snatcher," in *This Side of Doctoring: Reflections from Women in Medicine,* ed. Eliza Lo Chin (Thousand Oaks, CA: Sage Publications, 2001): 200.

8. "When Doctors Marry Doctors: A Survey Exploring the Professional and Family Lives of Young Physicians," Nancy W. Sobecks, Amy C. Justice, Susan Hinze et al., *Annals of Internal Medicine* 130, no. 4, part 1 (February 16, 1999): 312–19.

9. Ellen S. More, *Restoring the Balance: Women Physicians and the Profession of Medicine, 1850–1995* (Cambridge, MA: Harvard University Press, 1999).

10. Susan W. Miller et al., "The Impact of Divorce on Career Development," California Career Services, 2004.

11. Diary extract taken from Regina Morantz-Sanchez, *Sympathy and Science: Women Physicians in American Medicine* (New York: Oxford University Press, 1985): 307–8.

Elaine Stone

1. Simone de Beauvoir, *The Second Sex,* ed. and trans. H. M. Parshley (1952; New York: Knopf, 1953).

2. Robert L. Griswold, *Fatherhood in America: A History* (New York: Basic Books, 1993): 195.

3. Kate Millett, *Sexual Politics* (Garden City, NY: Doubleday, 1970).

4. Shuly Rubin Schwartz, *The Rabbi's Wife: The Rebbetzin in American Jewish Life* (New York: New York University Press, 2006).

5. Jill Abramson and Barbara Franklin, *Where They Are Now: The Story of the Women of Harvard Law 1974* (Garden City, NY: Doubleday, 1986).

A Note on the Author

Emma Gilbey Keller is the author of *Lady: The Life and Times of Winnie Mandela*. She has written for the London *Sunday Times*, the London *Daily Telegraph*, the *Guardian*, *Marie Claire, More* magazine, *Vanity Fair*, and *Tatler*, among others. She grew up in England and lives in New York City with her husband, Bill Keller, executive editor of the *New York Times*, and their two children.